# The Buddhist Art of Gandhāra

# The Buddhist Art of Gandhāra

The story of the early school
Its birth, growth, and decline

Sir John Marshall

Dev Publishers & Distributors

Published by
Dev Publishers & Distributors
Second Floor, Prakashdeep,
22, Delhi Medical Association Road,
Darya Ganj, New Delhi – 110 002

www.devbooks.co.in

ISBN: 978-93-81406-69-4

This Edition, 2018



Printed in India.

# CONTENTS

# LIST OF ILLUSTRATIONS

*The Plates are bound together between pp. 112 and 113*

LIST OF ILLUSTRATIONS

## LIST OF ILLUSTRATIONS

LIST OF ILLUSTRATIONS

# PREFACE

When Alfred Foucher wrote his masterly work on the Graeco-Buddhist art of Gandhāra, he laboured under one disadvantage: he had little external evidence to assist him in reconstructing the School's history and, though he was remarkably shrewd in his surmises, they sometimes went wide of the mark. Witness for instance his dating of the well-known statue of the Buddha in the Guides' Mess at Mardān (fig. 132 below), which he placed in the first century B.C.—two centuries before its actual date. Since Foucher's book was published, this dearth of chronological data has been in a large measure remedied by discoveries made in the course of my excavations at Taxila, which revealed many significant facts relating to the history of the School. Among the most important of these were the following: first, they established the fact that there were two distinct schools of art in Gandhāra, the earlier of which was flourishing in the first and second centuries of our era, the later in the latter part of the fourth and fifth centuries; and they also showed that these two schools were sharply distinguished, not only by the widely different character of their art but by the different materials which their sculptors employed, namely, stone in the case of the earlier school, lime-stucco in that of the later. It is with the earlier only of these two schools that we are here concerned.

Secondly, my discoveries showed that in the late Śaka period, to which the oldest examples of Buddhist carvings are referable, the old Hellenistic art in Gandhāra had sunk to a lamentably low level, though better work appears to have been done by sculptors of the Early Indian School imported from down country.

Thirdly, the new evidence from Taxila proves that a strong revival of Hellenistic art took place under the philhellene Parthians, who succeeded the Śakas in the North-West in the first century A.D., and that this Partho-Hellenistic art played an all-important part in the subsequent evolution of the Gandhāra School.

Fourthly, it is now abundantly clear that the Gandhāra School passed through its adolescence and maturity under the Kushāns, who overthrew the Parthians in *circa* A.D. 64, and that it came to an abrupt end in the reign of Vāsudeva I, when the Buddhist monasteries throughout the North-West were overrun and reduced to ruin.

Fifthly, it has also been made clear that different varieties of stone were in use at different periods in the School's history, and that the nature of their stones can help materially in determining the age of the sculptures.

With these leading facts established, the story of the School's development automatically resolved itself into three main chapters: its infancy under the Śakas; its childhood and early adolescence under the Parthians; and its later adolescence and maturity under the Kushāns. And when to this external evidence was further added the internal evidence of the sculptures themselves, the order of their sequence and the changing character of their successive styles at once became apparent.

This is the story that is unfolded in the following pages, and I am confident that in all essentials it will prove a reliable one. Let me make it plain, however, that I regard this little book as no more than a pioneer effort. I have laid the foundations and I believe them to be truly laid, but there is much to be done before the structure can be completed. Among other tasks, the stones used for these sculptures need to be examined and identified far more systematically than I have found possible. The quarries where the stones were hewn must also be located. Then the decorative patterns and other architectural features, as well as the fashions prevailing among celestials and mortals, need to be set out period by period. And these things cannot be done until the sculptures in the museums have been classified and catalogued afresh, and photographs in much larger numbers made available for study.

As to the scheme of the chapters, it should be noted (and I wish to emphasize this point) that the lines of demarcation between them are not to be regarded as clear-cut and precise. The process of evolution was continuous, and there are many sculptures which stand on the borderlines between two chapters and might justifiably be relegated to one side or the other. The problem, too, is complicated by the fact that the School of Gandhāra comprised several groups of ateliers at varying stages of development and with distinctive traditions and styles of their own. Nevertheless, taking Gandhāra art as a whole, I believe that the chapters into which I have divided its history will be found to be sufficiently accurate to fulfil their purpose.

For long I was hopeful that I should, myself, be able to carry out some of the tasks enumerated above, and I looked forward most of all to writing a companion volume which would deal with the Later School of Gandhāra on the same lines as this one deals with the Earlier. Declining health, however, coupled with rapidly failing eyesight have compelled me abruptly to desist from my labours and I must console myself with the hope that others may some time take up the threads of this research where I have had to drop them.

One other point. The main theme of this book is the history of Buddhist art in Gandhāra from a chronological and aesthetic, not from an iconographic, point of view. It was not, therefore, essential that I should explain the meaning of the many Jātaka and Life stories which occur among the reliefs and which occupy a substantial part of the text. I have done so, because I am well aware that relatively few readers are likely to be familiar with these stories and I believe that for the rest it will enhance the value of the illustrations if their meaning is explained. In this connexion I have made free use of the descriptions given in Alfred Foucher's work quoted above and in Harold Hargreaves's two catalogues of the sculptures in the Peshāwar and Taxila Museums; and I welcome this opportunity of acknowledging my indebtedness to these two distinguished authorities on Buddhist iconography.

It is also my pleasant duty to record my thanks to the Musée Guimet in Paris and to the museums of Lahore, Peshāwar, Simla and Calcutta for their generous gifts of photographs and for according me permission to publish them. And, finally, I have the rare privilege of thanking both the former Government of India and the Government of Pakistan for the generous help they have given in the production of this book—the former by enabling me to continue my archaeological work several years longer than would otherwise have been possible; the latter by making itself responsible for its publication.

J. M.

PUBLISHER'S NOTE

Sir John Marshall's death occurred before he had the opportunity to correct the proofs of this book, and it was seen through the press by the former Director of Archaeology in Pakistan, M. Raoul Curiel, and by Professor J. E. van Lohuizen.

# LIST OF ABBREVIATIONS

| | |
|---|---|
| *A.G.-B.G.* | *L'art gréco-bouddhique du Gandhāra*, by A. Foucher. Paris 1905–51. |
| *A.M.I.* | *Ancient Monuments of India*, by James Burgess. London 1897–1911. |
| *A.S.I.* | *Archaeological Survey of India.* |
| *A.S.R.* | *Annual Reports of the Archaeological Survey of India* (from 1902 onwards), ed. John Marshall and others. |
| *B.E.F.E.O.* | *Bulletin de l'École Française d'Extrême Orient.* |
| *B.M.* | British Museum. |
| *Cat.* | Catalogue. |
| *C.H.I.* | *Cambridge History of India.* |
| *C.I.I.* | *Corpus Inscriptionum Indicarum.* |
| *C.S.R.* | *Annual Reports of the Archaeological Survey of India* (1860–84), ed. A. Cunningham and others. |
| *I.M.* | Indian Museum. |
| *Ind.* | Indian. |
| *J.A.S.B.* | *Journal of the Royal Asiatic Society of Bengal.* |
| *M.I.C.* | *Mohenjo-daro and the Indus Civilisation*, by Sir John Marshall and others. |
| *Mon. Piot* | *Fondation Eugène Piot, Monuments et Mémoires publiés par l'Académie des Inscriptions et Belles-Lettres.* Paris. |
| *Taxila* | *Taxila*, by Sir John Marshall. 3 vols. Cambridge 1951. |

## CHAPTER I

# INTRODUCTION

For the information of those who may not be familiar with the word 'Gandhāra' let me start by explaining that it was the ancient name of the tract of country on the west bank of the Indus river which comprises the Peshāwar Valley and the modern Swāt, Buner and Bajaur. It was a country with rich, well-watered valleys, clear-cut hills and a pleasant climate: a country where a Greek might well dream of being back in his homeland. Situated on the borderland between India and Western Asia, Gandhāra belonged as much and as little to the one as to the other. In the sixth and fifth centuries B.C. it formed part of the Achaemenid empire of Persia. In the fourth it was occupied for a brief period by the armies of Alexander the Great. Thereafter it was conquered by Chandragupta Maurya, but after a century of Indian rule the West again asserted itself, and for another century (roughly, the second century B.C.) Greek dynasts took the place of Indian. Then came, early in the first century B.C., the victorious Śakas or Scythians, to be followed, after yet another century, by the Parthians and Kushāns. And even then the tale of foreign conquest was not ended. For in the third century of our era Gandhāra again reverted to Persia, now under Sasānid sovereigns, and was again reconquered by the Kidāra Kushāns in the fourth. Finally, the death-blow to its prosperity was given by the Ephthalites or White Huns, who swept over the country about A.D. 465, carrying fire and sword wherever they went and destroying the Buddhist monasteries.

With such a history behind them it is not surprising that the people of Gandhāra were thoroughly cosmopolitan in their culture and their outlook. Of their physical appearance we get some idea from the old sculptures. Some of the men, with strikingly tall and dignified figures, closely resembled many present-day Pathāns, and wore the same distinctive kind of baggy trousers and sleeved coat. Others were characteristically Greek; others just as characteristically Indian. And, no doubt, if we knew more about them, we should recognize other racial elements portrayed by the sculptors. The common speech of the people was an Indian Prākrit, but the script they used for the writing of this vernacular was not, as might have been expected, the current Brāhmī of Northern India but a script known as Kharoshṭhī—a modified form of the Aramaic of Western Asia, which had been adopted for official use throughout the Persian Empire during Achaemenid times. Other languages and other scripts were also employed, on occasion, in Gandhāra. The coins, for example, normally had Greek legends on their obverse, Kharoshṭhī on their reverse; but in rare cases the legends were in Brāhmī. Brāhmī, too, was the usual script employed in the sacred manuscripts of the Buddhists. Nevertheless it is true to say that Gandhāra took its everyday speech from India and its writing from the West. This intimate fusion of widely divergent elements was equally apparent in the religious life of the people. As each successive conqueror added his quota to the local galaxy of deities and creeds, the number and variety went on growing. In the second century A.D. the coins of the Kushān kings Kanishka and Huvishka, whose capital was at Peshāwar, exhibit a truly amazing gallery of gods and goddesses, unparalleled, I think, elsewhere in the field of numismatics. Most numerous are the Iranian types, including among others the sun (Mioro), the moon (Mao), the wind (Oado), fire (Athsho), war (Orlagno), victory (Oanindo). The names are given in corrupt Greek. The sun and moon also appear with the Greek labels of Helios and Salene [*sic*], the fire god with that of Hephaestos, while another Greek deity is Herakles. From the West, too, comes Anahita, the Babylonian Aphrodite, under the name of Nana or Nanaia; and from Egypt come Sarapis and Horus. Of Indian deities the most conspicuous are Śiva (Oesho) and the war gods, Skanda, Kumāra, Viśākha and Mahāsena (Skando, Komaro, Bizago, Maasena). To conclude that these multifarious deities were all worshipped at the heart of the Kushān empire in Gandhāra would be rash; for they may well have been designed as a means of popularizing the new gold currency in distant parts of the Kushān empire and even beyond its borders, where it was hoped the currency might compete with the Roman aureus. Indeed, the great predominance of Western Asiatic types on these coins suggests that the currency was intended for use in the West rather than in the East. But, however this may be, this gold coinage leaves us in no doubt that the attitude of the Kushāns towards religion was as thoroughly cosmopolitan as it was towards other matters, as cosmopolitan indeed as that of the Romans or Alexandrians, and perhaps no less practical. Looking at this coinage one would never guess that in the time of Kanishka and Huvishka Gandhāra and the greater part of the Kushān empire were overwhelmingly Buddhist.

The beginnings of Buddhism in Gandhāra go back no further than the middle of the third century B.C., when the Maurya emperor Aśoka sent one of his many missions to spread the gospel of his newly adopted faith among his subjects on the North-West frontier. Evidence of this mission's activities may still be seen in the fourteen Edicts of the emperor engraved on the rocks at Shāhbāz-Garhī in the Peshāwar Valley, which set forth the Buddhist principles of religion and ethic, and such simple rules of conduct as Aśoka deemed most conducive to the welfare of his people. To Aśoka also was due the outstanding importance of the stūpa or funeral mound as an emblem and cultural object of worship among the Buddhists. For one of the many acts by which he sought to popularize the Śākya faith was the gift to each of the principal cities in his dominions of a portion of the body relics of the Buddha. These he obtained by opening seven of the eight stūpas in which the relics had originally been enshrined and dividing up their contents. Along with the relics he also presented each city with a stūpa worthy of housing them. In making these gifts the emperor may well have recognized the value of providing the worshippers with some visible and tangible object on which to focus their thoughts and prayers. But, whatever his purpose, the effect of these relic-stūpas was profound and lasting. Not only did the presence of the relics make them cult objects of worship, but in after days the stūpa itself, whether it contained a relic or not, came to be regarded as a special symbol of Buddhism, worthy to be worshipped for its own sake; so that the mere erection of a stūpa, large or small and in whatever material, became an act of merit, bringing its author a step nearer salvation. This matter of the stūpa cult deserves our particular attention because it was on the adornment of the stūpa that the early Buddhists lavished the wealth of their sculpture, and stūpas, sometimes richly decorated, figure prominently among the reliefs of Gandhāra.

By the side of some of his relic-stūpas Aśoka also erected tall pillars of stone, crowned by lions or other symbolical animals and usually inscribed with one or more of his Edicts. These, too, came to be looked on as characteristic emblems of the Buddhist Church, and are frequently to be seen portrayed in the sculptured panels of the Early Indian and Gandhāra

Schools. The finest of the pillars were executed by Greek or Perso-Greek sculptors; others by local craftsmen, with or without foreign supervision.

How Buddhism fared under the Greek princes of the North-West during the second century B.C. is largely a matter of inference and surmise. For among the myriads of Buddhist monuments and antiquities that have survived until the present day there is not one that can be referred with certainty to Greek authorship in the second century before our era. Indeed, the only positive bit of information about this Greek period that we possess is the story told in the Milindapañha about king Menander and his conversion to Buddhism by Nāgasena. Though the story may be largely apocryphal, there is no reason for doubting its substantial truth. The Greeks were very open-minded about religious matters; and the teaching of Śākyamuni, by its essentially ethical character, by its logical reasoning, and by the stress it laid on free will and the observance of the golden mean, was bound to make a strong appeal to the Greek intellect, notwithstanding that it was based on a view of life altogether more negative and joyless than the Greek. Moreover, from a political point of view Menander must have had the strongest reasons for identifying himself with the Buddhist Church in its struggle against their common enemy, the Śunga king Pushyamitra, and the violent Brahmanical reaction championed by him, which had led to the wholesale destruction of Buddhist monasteries in the Eastern Panjāb.

In spite, however, of the general dearth of monumental or other evidence in regard to the Greek period, we shall be safe in concluding that Buddhism was a flourishing and powerful religion under Greek rule and in all probability supported by the State. This seems evident from the fact that the ruling families of the Śakas, who made it their policy to follow, wherever possible, in the footsteps of their Greek predecessors, lost no time in adopting Buddhism as their official religion. On the other hand, there are no grounds for supposing that the Greeks demonstrated their sympathy for Buddhism by erecting more memorials in honour of the Founder or by employing the resources of Greek art to embellish those already existing. It may well be that, so far as their adhesion to Buddhism had any but a political significance, they were mainly interested in the abstract doctrines of the great Teacher, and had little time or sympathy to spare for the cultural worship of a stūpa or the adoration of a lion-crowned pillar.

As to the material culture of the Greeks in this region, the available evidence goes to show that it was on the same general level as that of the Hellenistic world of the West. Thus, the Greek city of Sirkap at Taxila was laid out on the same chessboard pattern and fortified with the same kind of bastioned stone-walls as were then in vogue among Hellenistic town-planners elsewhere. And the Greek temple at Jaṇḍiāl outside the north gate of the Sirkap city exhibits a surprisingly pure type of Ionic capital, which in the second century B.C. would have done credit to an Athenian architect. But the stability and continuity of Greek art in Gandhāra and the North-West is best illustrated by the striking series of coins issued in those areas. These coins were not, be it said, up to the standard of the magnificent Greek coins of Bactria, unsurpassed by any in the ancient world, but they were well up to the average standard of contemporary Hellenistic coins in Western Asia, and they show that there were local coin engravers of ability capable of carrying on the art from generation to generation. That there were equally capable experts in other spheres of art need not be questioned.

When the Greeks were overcome by the Śakas, most of them doubtless stayed on, to live out their lives and bring up their families under alien rule. There could not, of course, be any question of their returning to the land of their forefathers in Bactria, since the Bactrian Greeks had long since been despoiled of their heritage by the Śakas. Doubtless it was some consolation to the Greeks in the North-West to know that their new masters had already come under the influence of Greek culture and familiarized themselves with the Greek way of life in Bactria, and that they could be counted on to continue the methods of administration established by the Greeks, to encourage Greek arts and crafts, imitate the local Greek coinage and in other ways follow their predecessors' example.

The Śakas themselves do not appear to have been a very artistic people. Here and there among their ornaments are some attractive examples of Scythic and, particularly, Sarmatian designs, but, with these few exceptions Śaka art in the North-West was nothing more than a perpetuation of decaying Greek art—so much so, indeed, that no one comparing, for example, the coins of the two peoples or taking note of the ornamental features of Śaka buildings, can doubt for a moment that the Śakas continued to employ the same Greek artificers as their predecessors, or that these artificers and their descendants were responsible for carrying on the Greek traditions to the last days of Śaka rule in the North-West. As the years went by, those traditions tended to grow weaker and the workmanship to deteriorate. That, indeed, was inevitable, seeing that the Śakas and their Greek subjects were almost entirely cut off by the Parthian empire from intercourse with the Western world. Later, when the Parthians themselves became masters of the North-West, Greek arts and crafts received a fresh and invigorating stimulus. For, like the Śakas, the Parthians were confirmed philhellenes and proud of their Hellenistic culture, and not only had they large numbers of Greek subjects in their empire but they were in a position to maintain close commercial contacts with the Mediterranean coasts. This revival of Greek arts and crafts is very noticeable at Taxila after its conquest by Gondophares, the Suren of Eastern Parthia. That an earlier revival had followed the transient victories of his predecessor Vonones is a possibility, but only a remote one. There is no evidence for it at Taxila. All the evidence from that site and all the evidence of the sculptures themselves go to show that at about the close of the last century before the Christian era there existed in Gandhāra local artists capable of turning out work in a decadent Hellenistic style which served at first as a basis for the incipient Buddhist art of that region, but that after the Parthian conquest of *circa* A.D. 25 there was a notable revival of Hellenistic art followed by a striking change for the better in the character of local Buddhist art. All this I shall discuss in detail in a later chapter. But first we must take stock of some artistic influences other than Greek which contributed to the making of the Gandhāra School, namely those of the Early Buddhist School of Central India and Hindustān.

CHAPTER 2

# THE EARLY INDIAN SCHOOL OF ART

(FIGS. 1–12)

We have seen that the earliest examples of Buddhist sculpture in stone date from the reign of the Maurya emperor Aśoka (274–232 B.C.), and that they were the handiwork of Greek or Perso-Greek sculptors assisted by local craftsmen. It should be emphasized, however, that it was not until a century later that stone came to be employed on at all a large scale in place of wood by the Buddhist sculptors of Central India and the Jumnā Valley; and it is reasonable, therefore, to suppose that the idea of using the less perishable material was borrowed from the Bactrian Greeks who were then established in the neighbouring kingdom of the Eastern Panjāb. Most important of the Buddhist monuments adorned in the new way were the early groups at Bhārhut, Sāñchī and Bodh-Gayā. Oldest among these are the balustrade and gateway of the Bhārhut Stūpa, which are assignable to the middle of the second century B.C. Then follow, in chronological order, the original carvings on the Second Stūpa at Sāñchī (*c.* 125 B.C.) and on the balustrade at Bodh-Gayā (*c.* 75 B.C.), the carvings on the four gateways of the Great Stūpa at Sāñchī (*c.* 50 B.C.), and, lastly, those on the gateway of the Third Stūpa at the same site, together with the later additions on the balustrade of the Second Stūpa, both of which are referable to the opening years of the Christian era. Thus, the age of this Early Indian School was comprised within the two centuries between 150 B.C. and A.D. 50, and it is important to note that it preserved its essentially Indian character unimpaired until the end.

The purpose of these sculptures was to glorify the Buddha. This they did by recounting episodes from the story of his life and of his previous births, or sometimes, but only rarely, from the subsequent history of the Buddhist Church. In the earliest monuments the stories of his previous births, or Jātakas, as they were called, greatly predominated. Later on, interest shifted to the events of his last earthly life, and still later to his image, which was destined to eclipse all else in Buddhist art. But that was not until the School of Gandhāra had initiated the idea and established the practice of portraying the Buddha in bodily form. In the Early

Indian School there is no trace of the Buddha ever having been so portrayed. In that School it was an inflexible rule that his presence should be indicated by means only of a symbol: by his footprints, for example, or his throne, or the promenade (*caṅkrama*) on which he was wont to take his daily exercise, or by his special bodhi tree, or his funeral mound (stūpa). This rule, which extended also to the Previous Buddhas, was religiously observed until the last days of the Early Indian School and was one of the chief characteristics that distinguished it from the School of Gandhāra.

At a very early stage in its history the Buddhist Church appropriated to itself many popular cults, folk stories and superstitions, as well as a variety of symbols of a quasi-religious order. Nor did it shrink from taking into its service and making free use of the popular, mundane, and often sensuous, art of the day. All this is clearly reflected in the sculptures of the Early School. Thus, the Jātaka stories, which play such an important role in the decorative scheme of the Bhārhut balustrade, were for the most part, as has long been recognized, nothing but old-time fables to which a new meaning had been given by the Buddhists. The large number of these stories at Bhārhut and the stereotype brevity with which they are recounted leave little room for doubt that they had long been a favourite theme among Buddhist sculptors before wood had been replaced by stone. Indeed, it is more than likely that they had been the common stock-in-trade of Indian sculptors before the days of the Buddha himself, which would account for the strangely anomalous rule of the Church which permitted the person of the Bodhisattva to be portrayed in the scenes of his former lives but not in those of his last one. We need not, however, delay longer over these or other early efforts of the Indian School, since for our present purpose they are less instructive than the later work of that School. Indeed, the only sculptures in this group which require our close attention here are those which were produced in the century between 50 B.C. and A.D. 50, and which were thus immediately antecedent to, or actually contemporary with, the beginnings of Buddhist art in Gandhāra. The finest of these sculptures are to be found on the four gateways of the Great Stūpa at Sāñchī and on the single gateway of the Third Stūpa (that of the Buddha's two chief disciples) at the same site. From them I have selected for illustration a dozen representative examples, which should suffice to give a fair idea of their style and workmanship and of the resemblances or contrasts which they offer with the sculptures of Gandhāra. And, first, let us look at a few examples of the symbolism which played such an important part in Buddhist iconography, and particularly so at this early period, when it was not yet permissible to depict the person of the Buddha.

The group in fig. 1 forms part of the crowning ornaments on the summit of the North Gateway of the Great Stūpa, the centre-piece of which (not included in the photo) is a *dharmacakra* or 'Wheel of the Law', of which more will be said anon. On either side of this Wheel and directly above the gateway jambs, stands a symbol of the *triratna* or 'Three Jewels'—the Trinity of Buddhism—and beside them an attendant *yaksha* holding a fly-whisk in their honour. The *triratna* or Three-Jewel symbol, derived from the older *nandipada* or 'taurine' symbol, was familiar at all ages on Buddhist monuments, but it was not always of the same form. Here, the wheel, centred with a lotus, must be taken to represent the *dharma* or Buddhist doctrine, the trident above it the Master, and the curious shield-like symbol in the centre (*śrīvatsa*) the Community (*saṅgha*). In some other examples of this symbol among the Sāñchī sculptures the 'shield' is omitted, and among the Gandhāra sculptures we shall find a whcel set on each of the Trident prongs (fig. 70), or the Trident replaced by three interlaced wheels (fig. 59). The figure of the attendant *yaksha*, let it be remarked, has a somewhat stiff and wooden appearance, in marked contrast with the free and supple figures in some of the reliefs, such as those in the right half of fig. 7. A point has been made of showing the *yaksha* from the back rather than the front because free standing figures are very rare among these sculptures as they are also in Gandhāra art. For other details, cf. Marshall and Foucher, *Monuments of Sāñchī*, pls. XXII, XXIV, XXVIII.

Another outstanding motif of Buddhist symbolism was the lotus, which is still the national flower of India. Thanks to the miracle of its own strange birth beneath the waters, it was pre-eminently the symbol of birth—particularly of divine birth. But it was more than that. It was also a 'Tree of Life and Fortune', and it is in this aspect of a 'wishing-tree' that it is so often depicted at Bhārhut and Sāñchī, laden with fruits and jewels and magic talismans—all symbolic of the countless blessings that Buddhism had to offer to mankind. A fine example of this lotus wishing-tree, carved on the lowest architrave of the Southern Gateway of the Great Stūpa, is reproduced in fig. 2. Here, the tree sprites, in the form of *kumbhaṇḍas*, are spouting out the lotus plants and their treasures as if spouting out summer itself, the plants and figures together making a pattern of singular richness and beauty, though one could wish perhaps that the snake-like convolutions of the lotus stems at the centre had been omitted. Parenthetically we should note that the *horror vacui*, the dislike of empty spaces, which distinguishes this design is characteristic of Indian decorative art throughout the ages, and is one of the chief features in which the sculpture of the Early Indian School contrasts with that of Gandhāra.

Owing to the ban imposed by the Buddhist Church on the representation of the Buddha's person, artists of the Early Indian School were hard put to it to illustrate the story of his last life. At first they confined themselves to portraying the four chief events in that life, namely, his Birth, his Illumination, his First Sermon, and his Death. Examples of these four events are reproduced in figs. 3, 4 and 5. The Birth they inevitably symbolized by a lotus plant, the traditional emblem, as already remarked, of miraculous birth; and to clarify the meaning, they sometimes added the figure of Māyā, the mother of the Buddha, either standing or seated on the lotus. In fig. 3 she is seated, a particularly comely figure, with two Nāga elephants pouring water over her from pitchers. The Illumination was represented by the pipal tree (*aśvattha*) in the shade of which it took place at Bodh-Gayā, sometimes with the seat of the Buddha at its foot (fig. 4*a*) sometimes enshrined in a temple with the armies of Māra on the one side and the heavenly hosts acclaiming the Buddha's victory, on the other (fig. 7). Of the First Sermon the recognized symbol was the 'Wheel of the Law' (*dharmacakra*), which the Buddha was figuratively supposed to have then set in motion and which has gone on revolving ever since. Sometimes the wheel was set on a throne or on the top of a pillar (in imitation of the pillar of Aśoka, erected on the spot where the sermon was preached) and frequently two or more deer were added, in allusion to the deer-park where this event took place (fig. 4*b*). Of the Death of the Buddha (*mahāparinirvāṇa*) the symbol, very appropriately, was the mound or stūpa in which his relics were enshrined (fig. 5).

These symbols of the four chief events in the Buddha's life were not inventions of the Buddhists. They had been associated with popular

Indian cults from time immemorial, and for that very reason had been annexed by the Buddhists and invested with a new significance. Thus the Sambodhi tree at Bodh-Gayā takes its place among the countless trees that from prehistoric days were objects of cult-worship in India, where every village had its sacred tree and every tree its living spirit. It was in the prehistoric age, also, that the wheel was invented, and we may well believe that it was not long before such a wonderful invention became an object of worship and was associated in men's minds with the sun's disk and the world-wide power which the sun typified. Even the two deer which the Buddhists used to symbolize the deer-park are figured on a prehistoric seal of the Chalcolithic Age. Lastly the funeral mound or stūpa had been the recipient of honours offered to the dead long before the death of the Buddha himself, though it was not until after Aśoka's nation-wide distribution of the Buddha's relics that the stūpa itself came to be universally adored in the Buddhist world.

In the mature reliefs of the Sāñchī gateways the four great events described above, as well as other episodes connected with the Buddha's last life or previous births, are sometimes depicted with a great wealth of imaginative and picturesque detail. A notable example is the Viśvantara Jātaka on the Northern Gateway, the second half of which is illustrated in fig. 6. In point of both style and technique it falls short of the best reliefs on these gateways, but it tells its story in simple, realistic language, like the language of some old tapestry, and succeeds in giving us a convincing glimpse of Indian jungle life. I have included it among my illustrations because it helps to demonstrate the width of the gulf which separates these sculptures of the Early Indian School from those of Gandhāra, and at the same time emphasizes the wholly different approach of the two Schools towards this kind of narrative relief-work. To appreciate my meaning, the reader has but to turn to fig. 130, to see how an artist of the Gandhāra School in its declining years set about illustrating this same Viśvantara Jātaka. Truly, it would be difficult to imagine a greater contrast!

Another notable example of the more elaborate sort of design to be found among the Sāñchī sculptures is the relief illustrating the Illumination scene on the lowest architrave of the Western Gateway (fig. 7). In the centre, the Buddha is represented by his throne beneath the bodhi tree, which by a strange anachronism is here shown growing through the roof of the hypaethral temple built around it in a later age by the Emperor Aśoka. To the right, the armies of Māra are in headlong flight after their vain assault and defeat by the Buddha. The scene is full of vigour and movement. The hurrying figures of bowmen and horsemen, the great elephant overtaking and trampling down the chariot in front of it, the demon in the foreground running his trident, somewhat humorously, into the back of his fallen comrade—all combine to make up a picture of panic-stricken rout and confusion, but without any sacrifice of rhythm and balance in the decorative scheme. To the left of the Bodhi Temple and in marked contrast with the scene on the right is a solemn and sedate procession of the gods, who with drums and banners and flower-offerings come to do honour to the victorious Buddha. The gods make a dull group, but the sculptor had no option in the matter. Whatever the occasion, the gods had to be portrayed as grave and stately beings, with stolid, unemotional countenances. That was the traditional rendering, to which the strictest regard had to be paid, and that is why the groups of heavenly *devas*, like the groups of earthly princes, invariably appear formal and stilted.

Yet another outstanding example of the mature Sāñchī style is reproduced in fig. 8. It depicts one of the lesser episodes in the Buddha's life, namely his meeting with his father Śuddhodana on his return to Kapilavastu and the miracle he performed on that occasion by walking in the air, followed by the gift to him of a banyan grove by his father. At the top of the panel is the familiar Conception scene, which here serves merely as a label to denote that the town portrayed is Kapilavastu. In the middle is a royal procession threading its way through the narrow streets of the town and out of the gate. At the bottom, in the foreground, the Buddha, represented by his promenade (*caṅkrama*), is seen walking in mid-air, while the king and his courtiers look up at him in wonderment. By the side of the royal group, in the left-hand corner, is a single banyan tree enclosed in a railing, to signify the banyan grove which Śuddhodana presented to his son. What concerns us here is not the story of the meeting but the way of telling it, so completely different from the way a Gandhāran artist would have done it. In spite of the awkward shape of the tall, narrow panel, the picture is delightfully free and unconstrained. The winding street, the houses with their crowded balconies, the royal chariot, the musicians in front of it, and the grand elephants, horsemen and bowmen behind: altogether a scene of the liveliest action and gaiety, a scene in which instinctive, unaffected artistry more than makes up for lack of proportion and perspective. And observe, too, near the top of the panel the realistic touch of the horse nuzzling into the neck of his companion, and the people in the balcony immediately below, whispering to one another about the passing show![1] The School of Gandhāra has nothing to show at all comparable to this sort of inborn, compelling artistry which seems to defy the limits of size and shape. The pity is that the sculptor felt bound to include the miracle at the base of the panel. He did all that could be done by placing the promenade among the tree tops and showing the upturned faces of the king and his retinue wondering at it: he can hardly be blamed if, artistically, the task proved an impossible one.

Besides the Jātaka fables and old world symbols described above there were many other religious elements handed down from earlier times which by a natural process of absorption became incorporated in the fabric of Buddhism. Thus, prominently featured among the early sculptures were the six Inferior or *kāmāvacara* heavens, with the gods who reside in them, including the Lokapālas, Yama, Śakra and Māra. Of the three heavens illustrated in fig. 9 the lowest is that of Yama, god of death; the next the Tushita heaven, where the Buddhas-to-be await the hour for their last coming to earth; and the uppermost the heaven of the Nirmāṇarati, who rejoice in their own creations. Each heaven is represented by the storey of a palace, in which sits a king with his viceroy on his right and the court musicians and dancers on his left, the same figures being repeated with slight variations in each of the heavens.

Fig. 10. The two reliefs of fig. 10, with their crowded scenes and almost bewildering details, are also telling examples of the same methods of composition. The story in the top panel (fig. 10*a*) is the well-known Śyāma Jātaka—the story of the young anchorite Śyāma, only son of a blind hermit and his wife, who is accidentally shot by the king of Benares on a hunting expedition. Though the several episodes are grouped in a single frame, the meaning is clear enough. In the centre, the figures of the king and the boy, who carries a pitcher on his shoulder, are a sufficient

[1] It is worth noting that one, if not two, of the figures in the lowest balcony on the right is wearing a wreath on his head. Evidently he is a foreigner from the North-West. Perhaps this was meant to be the Ambassadors' gallery!

label for identifying the Jātaka. Then, to the left, the figure of the king, now in hunting attire, twice repeated: first transfixing the boy with an arrow in the lotus pool, and then standing repentant with his bow by his side. On the banks of the pool, are cattle and deer and beyond them, to the right, the blind hermit and his wife seated in front of their huts. Finally, in the top left-hand corner, the father, mother and son (now restored to life through the intervention of the god Indra) are reunited in a happy group, together with the king and Indra himself. When we come to fig. 106, we shall have an opportunity of seeing how very differently the same Jātaka story was told by a sculptor of Gandhāra.

The panel below (fig. 10*b*) depicts the visit of the Nāga king Mucilinda to the Buddha soon after his Illumination. The Nāga king is seated in the foreground, with two of his queens on his right and a ballet troupe of dancers and musicians making up the rest of the Nāga group. In the background, behind Mucilinda, is the throne of the Buddha in the shade of a *nyagrodha* tree, which is attended by two *kinnaras* and two female celestials riding, respectively, on a winged lion and a griffin. Legend tells us that it was in the shade of a *nyagrodha* (*ficus indica*) tree that the Buddha rested in the fourth or fifth week after his Illumination, and it is interesting to observe the meticulous care with which the artist has depicted that particular species of fig-tree, in contradistinction to the *aśvattha* or *ficus religiosa* ordinarily associated with the Illumination.

Fig. 11 also gives us the same kind of crowded, animated scene—here a pleasure-retreat among rocks and waterfalls. In the foreground, ladies are bathing from the backs of elephants in a lotus-pool; to the left is a peacock; in the background, two amorous couples are seated in happy dalliance among the rocks, one of the males holding a drinking-cup, one of the females cooling her feet in the water. No doubt, this was one of the many genre scenes borrowed by the Buddhists from the mundane art of the day, and we can well believe that, like a well-known panel on the South Gateway, it was a work of ivory-carvers or inspired by an ivory prototype. But there is no reason to suppose that it served merely as a picturesque stopgap. That was not the way of the Buddhists. Admittedly, they were unashamed in appropriating popular mundane art (some of it of a flagrantly irreligious character) and flaunting it on their sacred monuments, but they never failed to invent new labels which would fit it into the Buddhist context. What new interpretation was put on this particular scene, we can only guess, but we may be sure that the setting for it was a celestial, not an earthly, paradise.

Fig. 12, the last of my Early Indian illustrations, shows one of the dwarf capitals of the Western Gateway. I have included it here mainly for the sake of comparison with the kindred Atlants of the Gandhāra School (cf. figs. 52, 70, 108, 145, 146). The Indian figures belong to the race of pot-bellied *kumbhaṇḍas* so familiar in Early Indian Art. Rough and uncouth as they may seem, they are the embodiment of energy and massive strength, and perfectly fulfil their architectural function of supporting the heavy gateway superstructure. Whoever was the sculptor, he certainly had a rare feeling for rugged strength and a rare genius for translating it into stone.

In concluding this all too brief sketch of the Early Indian School, there are three comments on its general character that deserve, I think, to be stressed. The first is that, notwithstanding the foreign elements that can be detected in it, it was essentially and indisputably Indian. Many of its motifs and ideas it borrowed from Western Asia, Assyria and Persia, still more of them from Greece; and to Greece also, or rather to the Hellenistic art of the North-West, it was indebted for valuable help in surmounting technical difficulties and thus smoothing the path of its development. But whatever these borrowings from outside sources, Indian art was able to assimilate them so thoroughly and organically that its own fundamental character remained unimpaired. As I see it, that character developed primarily from the deep, intuitive feeling of the Indian, especially the non-Aryan Indian, for rhythm and symmetry, coupled with his equally deep appreciation of plant and animal life and his unerring instinct for the stylization of form. These were factors that were common to every phase of ancient Indian art and which uniformly lay at the root of its beauty.

My second comment is that, although the art of this Early School was a religious art, initiated and developed under the aegis of the Buddhist Church, it was in fact based to a very large extent on the familiar mundane art of the period, only with such changes and additions—sometimes very slight ones—as were needed to give it its Buddhist complexion. This explains the presence on a Buddhist monument of such flagrantly sensuous scenes as those illustrated in figs. 11 and 12, which patently conflicts with the first principles of the Buddha's teaching. In such matters it seems to have been the Church rather than the artist who made the compromise. We shall see later that precisely the same thing happened in the case of Gandhāra art.

The final point I would stress concerns the startling disparity in the style and execution of many of these Early Indian sculptures. In some cases this disparity is of course due to the unequal ability of the sculptors responsible for the work, and nothing more need be said about it. But in other cases the disparity results from an over-conscientious regard for the traditional treatment of certain figures or groups of figures, particularly those of gods or earthly princes and their retinues. We have already seen a characteristic example of this in fig. 7, where the emotionless, puppet-like figures of the *devas* on the left, in violent contrast with the spirited scene on the right, are clearly due to established convention. The contrast is one that is constantly confronting us in these early sculptures.

CHAPTER 3

# THE BEGINNINGS OF GANDHĀRA ART: THE ŚAKA PERIOD

(FIGS. 13–28)

We have seen, in the first chapter, that Gandhāran art came into being in the last century before the Christian era, when the Śakas were ruling in the North-West and when the prevalent Hellenistic art which they had inherited from their Greek predecessors had already reached a decadent state. The character of this art and the way in which it declined under the Śakas and was subsequently given a new lease of life after the Parthian conquest is clearly apparent, albeit on a small scale, in a series of ornamental toilet-trays of Gandhāran workmanship which were unearthed in the Sirkap city at Taxila. They number thirty-three in all. Thirteen of them were of grey schist, twelve of micaceous or chloritized micaceous schist, four of steatite, two of claystone and two of slate. All these stones are found in their natural state in Gandhāra, but none of them in the neighbourhood of Taxila. Usually the trays are divided into two or more compartments and adorned with scenes or figures carved in relief. The subjects portrayed are few in number and all of a secular character. They comprise: a pair of lovers in an erotic scene; figure reclining on couch with attendant females; drinking and dancing scenes; male and female holding drinking-cups; lions, leogryphs, winged stags, hippocamps and the like with and without riders; and geometric and floral designs. Most of these subjects are clearly Hellenistic, and there can be no question that this type of toilet-tray was introduced with Hellenistic culture from the West, where numerous specimens have been found, especially in Egypt. Local influence, however, may possibly be seen in the lotus leaves or rosettes used as an accessory ornament and in the makara-like treatment of some of the sea-monsters.

Five of these toilet-trays from Sirkap are here illustrated (figs. 13–17). The oldest specimen was found in the fourth stratum (Early Śaka), but may well have been an heirloom from an earlier period. It is made of fine grey schist. Its style is distinctively Hellenistic and quite different from that of other trays of Śaka and Parthian times. On the rim is a beaded border encircled by a running spiral; in the centre, an erotic scene of a type familiar in Greek art, namely, a standing male figure wearing a hooded mantle of a pattern worn by Greek countrymen and, kneeling at his side, a woman wrapped in a *himation* or shawl, which her companion is pulling from her. The modelling of the figures, which are in high relief, is characteristic of Hellenistic sculpture and much superior to that of the other toilet-trays. On the back of the tray is a full-blown lotus in low relief.

The tray following (fig. 14) came from the fifth (Greek) stratum, but was doubtless a stray from above and referable to the latter part of the last century B.C. It is made of grey schist. The scene is a familiar Greek one, but the figures are very stiff and wooden by comparison with the preceding specimen. In the upper register is a man reclining on a couch with a wine-cup in his hand. At the head of the couch is a woman seated on a stool also holding a wine-cup; and behind the couch another woman standing up with a garland in her hand. The figures are clad in the Greek *chiton* and *himation.* In the lower register are seven palmette rays. Around the rim runs a beaded border in relief. Two features of the figures on this tray which merit special notice are the wig-like treatment of their hair and their wide-open, staring eyes. These features are found in several other trays dating from the late Śaka-Parthian period and they are peculiarly characteristic, as we shall see presently, of the earliest sculpture of Gandhāra.

The next tray (fig. 15) exhibits a fish-tailed hippocamp, with rider seated astride, and palmette rays in the exergue. Here, again, the rider is distinguished by the wig-like treatment of the hair and wide-open, prominent eyes. Found in Stratum 2, and referable to the Late Śaka period.

Fig. 16 is the most elaborate of all the toilet-trays. Unlike the foregoing examples, it is made of greenish-grey steatite (soapstone). Round its rim is a border of double arcading; in the centre, a drinking scene. At the top a man and woman are seated on a bench, the former clasping his companion with his left arm and holding a sceptre with his right, while she offers him a cup of wine. To the left of them is a draped woman, seated and playing on a lyre, and behind her a youth playing on the Pan-pipes. To the right, a standing male figure holding a staff in his left hand. In the middle register, to right, a large winevat, rising from acanthus leaves, in which two men, one on the back of the other, are treading grapes, while a lad in the centre draws off the juice in a tall flagon. To the left, another man is carrying a wineskin on his back and emptying its contents into a *krater*, while his companion on the left of the vase is raising a bowl to his lips. Below, in the bottom register, two figures are lying drunk. Framing the top of the scene from side to side is an undulating vine. The style is typical of Hellenistic art of the first century A.D., and the scene is reminiscent of the 'Wedding of Ariadne and Dionysus'—a familiar subject to Graeco-Roman art. A feature of this tray that should be specially noticed is the figure of the woman seated beside her companion on the bench, with bared back and prominently developed buttocks. This particular type of female figure occurs in other reliefs of the Parthian period, but is not, so far as I know, found in later Gandhāra work (cf. figs. 17, 18 and 51).

Fig. 17 is also of steatite and of approximately the same date as the foregoing. In the upper register is a sea-monster ridden by a half-draped female holding a baby in her left arm. In exergue, acanthus leaf in low relief. On the back, Kharoshṭhī inscription *Maṁjuminasa*. The treatment of the female rider, half-clad and with bared back and prominent buttocks, closely resembles that of the preceding example, though the workmanship is coarser.

As a supplement to the above samples of trays from Sirkap, I append another interesting example (fig. 18) from Narai village in the Peshāwar District, which in 1928 was in the possession of Mr L. W. Jardine, Assistant Commissioner of Mardān. The yellow stone of which it is made is said to come from a quarry beyond Dakka on the Jalālābād Road. The scene of the three winged Erotes, the irate Aphrodite giving a drubbing to one of them, and the half-length statue supported on a low pillar, are typical of the comic Alexandrian style. Observe that in this example also the half-draped female with bared back and prominent buttocks is of the same stock type as those in figs. 16 and 17 above and fig. 51 below.

The renaissance of Hellenistic art under the Parthians played such a momentous part in the evolution of the Gandhāra School that we shall have to return to the subject again in the next chapter and discuss it in greater detail. Meanwhile there remains to be noticed a number of other pieces of Gandhāran sculpture in the late Śaka style as well as two statues of local manufacture dating from the opening years of the Christian era. All the Gandhāran pieces are made of the micaceous or chloritic micaceous stone found West of the Indus; the two local statues of the Tarakī sandstone quarried in the neighbourhood of Taxila.

The small female statuette in the round (fig. 19) comes from the third stratum in Sirkap and is referable to the latter part of the last century B.C. The pose is rigidly frontal, with feet and legs together and hands on hips. The figure is nude except for ornaments, which consist of anklets, girdle, crossed breast-chain, armlets and bangles. The hair which is treated like a wig in front, is taken back from the forehead and falls in a long double plait down the back, with a few curls on each shoulder. On the top of the head is a low *polos*. Beneath the small base is a tenon, evidently intended to fit into a socket-hole. In ancient times the statuette was broken into two at the knees, and, in order to repair it, two holes were drilled between the legs, one above and one below the fracture. That the statuette may have served as a miniature Caryatid is suggested by the tenon under the base and the *polos* on the top of the head; and this would explain its unusually stiff, frontal pose, From the peculiar, wig-like treatment of the hair and the wide-open, staring eyes it is evident that this statuette is of the same age as the late Śaka toilet-trays (e.g. fig. 14), in which these features occur.

The other female statuette (fig. 20) is made of the same variety of stone and is approximately of the same age, but is modelled with relative freedom and not a little grace. The figure is nude save for a shawl or *sārī*, which falls over the left arm and below the hips in front. The left hand holds the hem of the *sārī*; in the right hand, which is raised to the breasts, is a lotus. Her ornaments consist of a hip-girdle; a breast-chain, crossed both front and back; bracelets; armlets; a narrow *taenia* across the forehead; and a medallion at the back of the head. The hair is taken back from the forehead and falls in a long double plait down the back, with a few curls on the shoulders. As usual at this early period, the eyes are large and staring, their pupils marked with a drill point. But there is much greater freedom in the treatment of the hair than in figs. 14 or 19, for example. The modelling of the head and torso and arms shows considerable feeling for form. The folds of the drapery are delineated by incised lines—a feature that is very characteristic of this period of

Gandhāra sculpture. The type appears to be derived from a Greek Aphrodite type, but is much Indianized. Probably it represents the goddess holding a lotus in her hand, who is portrayed on certain autonomous coins of Taxila and may be intended for Māyā, the mother of the Buddha (*B.M. Cat. Ancient Indian Coins*, pl. XXXII, 5, 6). Figures in the round are very rare in the Gandhāra School and almost exclusively of early date. This statuette was found in Block D′, Stratum II, in company with 102 copper dies and ornamental objects. Like so many other treasures found in Sirkap, the deposit was buried at the time of the Kushān invasion soon after A.D. 60, but it should be observed that the statuette had suffered much wear and tear before it was buried, and its date must be substantially earlier.

Whether the above figure is to be identified with Māyā or not, there is no question about the Buddhist character of a group of small stūpa-brackets emanating from the Sirkap site as well as from some of the Buddhist *saṅghārāmas* at Taxila. Though insignificant objects in themselves, these brackets are instructive. In the second and first centuries B.C. the Buddhists of Hindustān and Central India made a practice of providing their stūpas with brackets on which swags and garlands could be hung. These brackets, which went by the name of *nāgadanta*, were set at regular intervals round the dome of the edifice, a few feet above the base. If the reader will turn back to fig. 5, he will see them clearly delineated. In the Buddhist architecture of Gandhāra brackets were employed for the same purpose, but in Gandhāra they assume a much more elaborate form, being enriched generally with the figures of winged *devas* who, as in fig. 5, are supposed to be bringing offerings to the stūpa. A stūpa with brackets of this kind still in position was unearthed at Chakpat in Swāt and is illustrated in Foucher, *A.G.-B.G.* vol. I, figs. 10–12, pp. 56–9. The specimens from Sirkap are all of chloritic micaceous schist and date from about the beginning of the Christian era or a little later, when the Graeco-Śaka art was in a degenerate state. The modelling is clumsy, the chiselling coarse and careless, and the figures display the same prominent eyes and the same rough delineation of the drapery folds that are to be seen in other contemporary carvings. From the Indian dress and ornaments which the *devas* are wearing it is clear that they are copied from Indian prototypes. Let it be noted, too, that in the early examples there is nothing Hellenistic in the design of the bracket, but in the later ones a touch of Western influence can be seen in the acanthus base from which the figures spring as well as in the volute-like form of the bracket itself.

A typical specimen of the earlier brackets is fig. 21, which takes the form of a winged *deva*, with hands in front of breast, holding an uncertain offering. The *deva* is wearing bangles, long and short necklaces, and a shawl, which is drawn across the back and through the arms, leaving the front of the body bare. On the head is a broad, tasselled bandeau. The legs are missing from below the knees. Observe the roughness of the modelling, the careless portrayal of the folds of the shawl, and the wide-open, prominent eyes.

In the following example (fig. 22) the *deva* is shown emerging at the hips from an acanthus leaf base, and wearing a sleeved tunic, shawl and native turban, with cylindrical ear-ornaments of local pattern. His two hands are raised in adoration in front of his breast. On the back and on the tenon at the base of the bracket is a Kharoshṭhī inscription: *savatrateṇa niyatito vihare matapitu puyae devadato* ('Presented by Sarvatrāta in the Vihāra, in honour of his mother and father, Devadatta'). On palaeographical grounds the lettering is referable to the first half of the first century A.D. This volute shape and the acanthus motif at the base are Hellenistic features which mark a somewhat later date than the preceding example, and taken as a whole the design is good, but the execution is disfigured by the same clumsy modelling and careless, unsteady chiselling that characterize other sculptures of this period. The bracket was found in Stratum II, Block J, of Sirkap.

The three following examples from Buddhist sites at Taxila are of somewhat later date than the foregoing and carved from different varieties of stone. They show an increasing elaboration of detail and a progressive improvement in the modelling and execution, for which the Hellenistic revival under the Parthians may have been responsible.

In fig. 23, the winged *deva* is emerging, like the last, from an acanthus leaf base. He wears a *dhoti*, scarf and turban, with a large central ornament, heavy ear-rings, jewelled collar and long flexible necklace. His left hand grasps the scarf hanging over the left shoulder; his right rests on the hip. The bracket at the back is fashioned to resemble a serpent with scaly surface and double head. Although the design and technique are more advanced than in the preceding specimens, the eyes are still unduly wide-open and large, and the folds of the scarf are indicated by roughly incised lines.

The following example (fig. 24), which is now in the British Museum, came in all probability from the Dharmarājikā, where also the head of an almost identical bracket was found. Both are made of a talcose schist of a peculiarly silky texture. The *deva* is wearing a *dhoti*, scarf and turban, heavy ear-rings, short necklace, armlets and bangles. As a whole, the bracket is well designed and the modelling of the face is unusually good, but the treatment of the shawl and *dhoti* is still very perfunctory. For a similar bracket from the Dharmarājikā see *Taxila*, pl. 226, no. 167.

Another stūpa-bracket of the same class, but of more advanced style, is made of quartz-schist and is adorned with a female deity (*devī*), instead of a *deva* (fig. 25). The *devī* wears a close-fitting, long-sleeved garment, large circular ear-ornaments, flat collarette, long flexible necklace and bangles. In front of her breasts she carries an offering of fruit or flowers in both hands. The hair on the forehead is confined by a *taenia*, behind which it falls backward in long tresses and plaits over the shoulders. In the centre, above the *taenia*, is a circular medallion. The volute bracket is enriched with acanthus foliage on its sides and front. The eyes are still unduly large, but the modelling of the torso is more mature than in the preceding examples. The use of quartz-schist also points to a somewhat later date—probably the third quarter of the first century A.D. Not long after that date this type of stūpa-bracket appears to have gone out of fashion, as no later examples are known.

There remains one more of these early Gandhāra sculptures from Taxila, which is in a class by itself (fig. 26). It is made of micaceous schist and was found on the Sirkap site. Its special value lies in the fact that it is the oldest of all the pictorial reliefs of the Buddhist School of Gandhāra, and that the composition and handling of the figures show the closest dependence on the Early Indian School. The Jātaka story which it illustrates has not yet been identified. In the foreground a young anchorite is being borne along, suspended head downwards, on a pole which is carried on the shoulders of two of his companions. Looking on from the background are five other anchorites, the one on the extreme right headless. All have long hair and are distinguished by their staring eyes. Two are young and clean-shaven, one is bearded, another wears a moustache. The one on the left holds a flask in his left hand. Two of the older men have spotted deer-skins over their left shoulder. All appear to have the right hand upraised in front of the body, the centre one holding it against his right shoulder, palm inwards. The pole-carrier on the right wears a short skirt, the left one is defaced. The suspended figure grasps the pole with his two hands, with his knees around the pole and his feet extended upwards. There are traces of another figure behind the pole-carrier on the right.

That this relief is a product of the Gandhāra School is proved by the variety of local Gandhāra schist of which it is made; and that it dates from the late Śaka period is suggested by the character of the carving and the peculiarly distinctive treatment of the hard, staring eyes of the anchorites. In the case of the stūpa-brackets of this early period, we have seen that the Gandhāra sculptors made use of Indian models for their winged *devas*, and then proceeded to elaborate them with the Greek volute bracket and acanthus foliage, thus giving the design a definite hybrid character. In this Jātaka relief there is no trace of any Hellenistic features. It appears to be the handiwork of a sculptor who was trained in the Early Indian School but had adopted, in Gandhāra, the local method of treating the eyes. Even at this early stage the relief foreshadows the all-important part which religion was destined to play in the transformation and development of Gandhāra art.

In concluding this chapter on the art of the late Śaka period, it remains to notice two other pieces which, though unconnected with the Gandhāra School, have a definite bearing on the history of the Buddha image—a subject on which we shall have much to say later. Both sculptures (figs. 27 and 28) are made of a fine-grained sandstone from Tarakī in the neighbourhood of Taxila, which is the same stone as that used in the building of the Greek temple at Jaṇḍiāl and in the Śaka-Parthian palace in Sirkap, and since the very few sculptures made of this stone are in a distinctive style of their own, it is natural to conclude that they were the work of a small local School at Taxila. One of the statues (fig. 27) was found in Sirkap. It is a male figure wearing a tunic tied by a cord at the waist and reaching to the knees, a long shawl or *chlamys*, and high boots. The hair is dressed in the wig-like fashion that is characteristic of some of the statuettes and toilet-trays of late Śaka date described above. The heavy, uncouth modelling of the limbs must be largely due to the nature of the sandstone, which does not lend itself to fine work. Although free-standing, the statue is treated in the flattened manner of an alto-rilievo. The right forearm, which was attached by means of a tenon and socket, is missing and the face is completely mutilated. In the treatment of the shawl, which falls loosely round the shoulders and arms and stands out on either side of the hips, the statue bears a close resemblance to the so-called Hermes on a coin of Azes II (*B.M. Cat.* pl. XIX, 1). The high boots which the figure is wearing suggest that it may represent Sūrya, the sun-god, whose temple is said by Philostratus (*Life of Apollonius*, ii, 24) to have stood in the city of Sirkap.

The other statue (fig. 28), which is in the same broad, massive style, was unearthed at the Dharmarājikā and is, therefore, unquestionably Buddhist. The figure, which is 16 in. high, is wearing a *dhoti*, shawl and bracelets. The left hand rests on the hip; the right is raised in front of the breast with the fingers in what is known as the *chin-mudrā* or *jñāna-mudrā*, denoting meditation, knowledge and purity. The head and feet are missing. Although the statue is ostensibly in the round, the back is not modelled and the front is flattened as in a relief. In spite of its relative coarseness, the broad, massive style lends an impressive dignity to this image, which was wanting in the preceding one. Both, however, belong to the late Śaka period, and we shall probably not be far wrong if we assign them to the first quarter of the first century A.D. That the image represents the great Teacher himself can hardly be questioned, and the bracelets on his wrists might be taken to show that it represents him as the Bodhisattva, not as the Accomplished Buddha. But the image, be it remembered, dates from a time when the canonical types of the Buddha and Bodhisattva had not yet been fixed, and it may well be that the figure is intended to portray the Buddha after his Enlightenment. In any case, it is the earliest image of Gautama now known to us.

CHAPTER 4

# THE RENAISSANCE OF HELLENISTIC ART UNDER THE PARTHIANS AND ITS EFFECT ON GANDHĀRA ART

(FIGS. 29–39)

The Śakas and Parthians were alike in being philhellenes, admirers of Greek institutions and of Greek material culture. But the Śakas in the North-West had the misfortune of being cut off by the Parthian Empire from intercourse with the centres of living Hellenism in Western Asia, and in their isolation were unable to sustain the relatively high quality of the art which they had inherited from their Greek predecessors. The Parthians, on the other hand, not only had vast numbers of Asiatic Greeks within the borders of their own Empire, but were able to enjoy at least in times of peace both commercial and cultural contacts with the Graeco-Roman world. Thanks to this, Hellenistic art, as the Parthians knew it in the first century of our era, was still a living and progressive art, far superior to the lifeless and decadent kind of art then in vogue among the Śakas. Parthian art was in fact part and parcel of the Hellenistic art then prevailing in the West of Asia. Of this the Parthian remains at Taxila have furnished many proofs, including objects of stone, terracotta, metal, gold and silver jewellery, silver and bronze vessels, engraved gems and seals. Many of the smaller articles may have been imported from the West, but others were undoubtedly made on the spot. Of the former I shall content myself with giving three examples, figures 29, 30 and 31. The first of these is a head of Dionysus or Silenus in silver repoussé (fig. 29). The head of the god is bald on top and wreathed with a grape-vine. His ears are pointed. In his right hand he holds a two-handled wine-cup (*kantharos*). Behind his head passes the curved staff (*thyrsos*), with a bell suspended at its end. The relief once stood on a small stand, which was found separately. It closely resembles the handle of a *kylix* and was probably made for that purpose. The relief-work is very deep (1·35 in.) and the style and workmanship first-class. The *kantharos* is of a type which was in vogue about 300 B.C., and it is possible that the relief was an antique of that date. On the other hand, it may be a copy of earlier work. In favour of the former hypothesis is the fact that among the jewellery with which it was found was a gold and lapis-lazuli finger-ring of an earlier period, though not so early as 300 B.C.

The next example, fig. 30, is a bronze statuette of the Egyptian child-god Harpocrates, offspring of Isis and Osiris. Cast solid, probably in a piece-mould, the child-god stands with heels almost together, wearing a long sleeveless tunic, which reaches to his ankles and leaves his left shoulder bare. His right forefinger is raised towards his lips—a gesture which the Greeks and Romans interpreted as enjoining silence upon his votaries, who were forbidden to speak of the mysteries revealed to them, but which seems rather to have been a natural gesture of childhood. In his left hand he held some object which has disappeared—possibly a lotus, symbol of resurrection, or a cornucopia, symbol of the fruitfulness of nature which he personified. His hair, which is waved from the centre, falls in a long tress on his right shoulder. On his head he wears the Egyptian crowns of the North and South. The statuette is a typical piece of Graeco-Roman bronze-work, which may well have come from Alexandria, where the cult of Harpocrates was centred, though such statuettes appear to have been made in many parts of the Graeco-Roman world. As a work of art, it is not on a high level. The statuette was unearthed beneath the floor of a room in Block E, Stratum II, of Sirkap. Just below it was found an earthenware pot containing a valuable hoard of jewellery and other objects.

The third example (fig. 31) is the head of a female figurine of buff-coloured terracotta. She wears an open-work net, perhaps of gold or silver, over the front of her hair and a high bandeau behind, with a rosette above the left ear. The modelling is delicate and sensitive. It is referable to the first century A.D.

The three samples given above may well have been, like many other small *objets d'art*, imports from the Near East. But that Taxila could boast of competent artists capable of executing equally good work is proved by a number of stucco sculptures found in the great Buddhist Apsidal Temple in Sirkap. This temple was erected on the remains of buildings overthrown by the earthquake of *circa* A.D. 30, and was destroyed some thirty years later by the invading Kushāns. It was built on an imposing scale in the new kind of diaper masonry which was introduced from Gandhāra for the first time after the earthquake as being more stable than the traditional rubble. That the main building would take several years to complete, and that the two stūpas in its courtyard would not be added until after its completion, may be taken for granted. The date of the main building must be about A.D. 40 and the stūpas a few years later.

For the decoration of the stūpas the architects made use of small figural reliefs in stucco, numerous heads of which were found lying in the debris. Of the structures themselves from which they had fallen nothing unfortunately has survived, and we are left, therefore, to guess at the disposition and design of the decoration. One thing, however, is clear, namely, that the Buddhists of Taxila were as quick to make use of the newly revived Hellenistic art as the Buddhists of Gandhāra were. Some typical examples of these heads are illustrated in figs. 32–7. A few of them, like figs. 32 and 33, are plainly Hellenistic types, and modelled, moreover, by a sculptor of considerable ability and feeling for form. Others are inferior in style and execution and may be presumed to be the work of local craftsmen working under his supervision. At one time I took the view that figs. 32 and 33 might have been fashioned with the help of moulds imported from Western Asia. But closer study has shown me that this view is not really tenable. If the reader will look at the examples illustrated he will see that, while some of them, like figs. 33 and 37, were evidently intended to be seen full-face, others, like figs. 32, 35 and 36, were intended to be seen three-quarter face with one or the other cheek turned towards the wall to which the head was affixed. In the case of such three-quarter reliefs the sculptor was naturally prone to carelessness when fashioning the side of the face hidden from the spectator. Countless examples of this defect can be seen among the stucco reliefs at Jauliāñ and other fourth–fifth century sites, the carelessness being most marked in those of poorest quality. The same is true of the reliefs from the Apsidal Temple. Thus in figs. 35 and 36, which are inferior pieces of work, the distortions of the features on the unseen side of the face are very pronounced. On the other hand, in the Satyr's head, fig. 32, which is the work of a competent artist, the difference between the two sides is not so marked, but it is quite marked enough to leave us in no doubt that the sculptor must have done his modelling of this head in the position in which it was to remain against the face of the stūpa wall, and that he must have done it without the help of a mould; for had a mould been employed, we may be sure that both sides of the head would have shown the same amount of care and precision. For a highly elaborate and deeply undercut head of this kind, a piece-mould would, of course, have been needed, and there is no evidence that piece-moulds were used at Taxila for stucco reliefs of this kind, though they must have been used for the solid casting of objects in the round.

We must conclude, then, that all these reliefs without exception were modelled by hand on the spot, the best of them by a sculptor familiar with Hellenistic ideals and methods, the rest by local craftsmen of varying ability. It may be recalled that the same thing had happened in the case of the famous pillars of Aśoka, erected nearly three centuries earlier. Two of them, at Sārnāth and Sāñchī, are magnificent specimens of Hellenistic sculpture, executed by a master of the art; the others, of different degrees of merit but all much inferior, are evidently the works of his local assistants. That skilled artists and craftsmen from Western Asia were being encouraged at this time to find work under Parthian patronage at Taxila is evidenced by the well-known story of St Thomas. According to this story, the apostle, who was a carpenter or builder by trade, was recruited in Syria by an Indian merchant named Habban to accompany him to India, to take service at the court of the Parthian king Gondophares, for whom he was acting as agent. Whatever the precise facts behind this story, it fully confirms the conclusion drawn from the monuments themselves that the Parthian conquest of the North-West and the consequent opening-up of communications with the Mediterranean coasts were followed by an influx not only of small *objets d'art* from Western Asia and Egypt but also of artists and skilled craftsmen seeking their fortunes under the patronage of the philhellene Parthians. We shall see presently that further evidence on this subject is provided by sculptures from the Peshāwar Valley.

The Satyr head referred to above (fig. 32) has typical pointed ears, broad flat nose, moustache, beard and free-flowing locks. There is nothing mechanical or crude about the workmanship. There is an intensity of expression in the knitted brows and half-parted lips and a boldness in the treatment of the hair and beard that bespeak a thorough mastery over the material, coupled with a proper understanding of its limitations. The strong, almost portrait-like individuality that characterizes the countenance is typical of Greek art in its later phases; it is never found in early Indian art; nor is it a characteristic of the Gandhāra School.

The next head (fig. 33) is also truly Hellenistic. It, too, is bearded, but the beard is treated in even simpler masses, and there is a quiet dignity and repose about the features that find their nearest parallel among cult statues of the Greek pantheon. Unfortunately, the upper part of the head is mutilated, but what remains is quite enough to show that the sculptor had an intimate knowledge of Hellenistic art and complete command of his material. In fig. 34, a female head with heavy wreath, the hair is parted from the centre and rolled back over the ears, with two rosettes on the left side. The right side of the forehead and part of the nose are damaged. The wreath and top-knot (which is here mutilated) were very fashionable at this period. The small, pretty features call to mind those of contemporary terracotta figurines.

The remaining three heads are less successful. The bearded head (fig. 35) is very sketchily drawn, with deep-set eyes, overhanging brows and long, oval face. It was intended to be seen three-quarter face and its left side was carelessly modelled. The top of the head and ears are missing. In the following example (fig. 36)—a female head with highly arched brows and slightly smiling lips—it is the right side of the head which was turned away from the spectator and is hence carelessly modelled. In contrast with these two heads, the next one (fig. 37) was all but full-face and there is little difference in the modelling of the two sides. This head and figs. 34 and 36 illustrate, though not as clearly as some other terracotta and stucco heads from Taxila,[1] the form of indoor head-dress in vogue among the Parthian nobility, namely, a chaplet (of Hellenistic origin) with the long hair dressed as a top-knot inside it. Both of these features—the top-knot and the chaplet—seem to have been recognized as symbols of aristocratic birth and this no doubt explains why from this time onwards images of the Buddha were habitually provided with such a top-knot, under the name of *ushṇīsha*.[2]

Besides these stucco figures in the Hellenistic style and somewhat feeble imitations by local craftsmen, there are a few heads of the Bodhisattva belonging to the same group from the Apsidal Temple. One of them (fig. 39) must have belonged to a statue of superhuman size. Cunning-

[1] E.g. *Taxila*, vol. III, pl. 138*a*, and pl. 148, 4, 7, 9.
[2] E.g. figs. 61, 63, 66, 67 below.

ham records that, when clearing the nave of the Apsidal Temple in 1863 (*C.S.R.* v, p. 74), he found numerous pieces of burnt-clay statues of colossal size, which had stood against the walls of the nave. Large statues in such a position, where they were protected from the weather, would normally be made of clay, and would, of course, be converted into terracotta, if the building happened to be burnt down. On the other hand, statues intended for a more exposed position would be made of the more durable stucco. It is reasonable, therefore, to infer that the statue we are discussing probably stood in the shallow entrance porch to the temple, where it would not be entirely protected from the rain. That it was the work of one of the local craftsmen engaged on these sculptures and that it represents the Bodhisattva in princely attire can hardly be questioned. Thus it has the distinction of being the earliest known head of the princely type of Bodhisattva which was afterwards to become the standard type of Gandhāra.

The small head of the Bodhisattva illustrated in fig. 38 wears a moustache, ear-pendants (right one missing) and elaborate turban. The turban is in three rolls, crossing in the middle of the forehead and finished with a fan-tail ornament above. The left side of the face is more roughly modelled than the right.

The colossal head referred to above (fig. 39) was similar in appearance to the foregoing but on a larger scale. The modelling is rough and devoid of feeling. The moustache, which is missing, was affixed separately.

It remains to add that the stucco of which all these figures were made is composed of lime mixed freely with small broken stone (*bajrī*) and other foreign matter. It is coarser than the stucco used on the later monuments of the fourth and fifth centuries; nor is there any trace of the fine finishing coat which was used to embellish some of the later stuccos. At Taxila there is no evidence of stucco of any kind having been used for figural work before the Parthian period. I purposely use the word 'figural', because there is one small stūpa in Sirkap dating from pre-Parthian times which is decorated with a design of acanthus foliage worked out in a thick coat of stucco. This is the stūpa brought to light in Court *a* of Block E, and described and illustrated in *Taxila*, vol. I, p. 158 and vol. III, pls. 27*a* and 120A. From the level at which it stood, this stūpa would appear to have been contemporary with the small Śaka stūpas at the Dharmarājikā referable to the latter part of the first century

B.C.; but in this case it is more than likely that the stucco decoration was added after the Parthian occupation of Taxila, but before the great earthquake of *circa* A.D. 30, when the stūpa was lifted bodily from its base and turned almost upside down before being buried in the ruins of the surrounding buildings.

These illustrations will, I hope, suffice to show the high quality of the revived Hellenistic art which the Parthians introduced at Taxila and the influence which it exercised on the local Buddhist School. We have now to go westward across the Indus, and see what effect its impact had upon the Buddhist School of sculpture in Gandhāra.

## CHAPTER 5

# CHILDHOOD OF GANDHĀRA ART

(FIGS. 40–52)

The artists of the Early Indian School in Mālwā who were commissioned to carve the gateways of the Great Stūpa at Sāñchī, did not hesitate to include among their reliefs scenes of a sensuous and erotic character which were flagrantly opposed to the first principles of Buddhist teaching. With such a well-established precedent to guide them, it is not surprising that, after the revival of Hellenism under the Parthians, the sculptors of Gandhāra followed a like course. At that time a favourite theme of Graeco-Parthian secular art was the drinking-scene, and incongruous as it may seem, this was one of the earliest themes to be adopted for the decoration of Buddhist stūpas. At the outset such themes were incorporated, just as they were and without any modification, among the stūpa-reliefs, though no doubt appropriate labels, based on one or other of the life-stories of the Buddha, were readily invented for them. But it was evidently not long before doubts began to arise as to the propriety of these drinking-scenes on the walls of sacred edifices, and so we find the sculptors giving them a more sober and holier air by putting lotuses instead of wine-cups in the hands of the revellers. The change was a simple and effective one, but it is worth remarking that the drinking-scene was much too popular to be so easily suppressed or camouflaged. We find it recurring time and again in later reliefs of the Gandhāra School.

A good illustration of such scenes, of a purely Hellenistic character, is afforded by fig. 40. This relief was formerly in the Guides' Mess at Mardān and like the majority of their sculptures probably came from Swāt; but its precise provenance is uncertain; nor have I been able to ascertain the variety of stone of which it is made. It is now in the Peshāwar Museum. The drinking party comprises nine figures, namely, four male and five female. The men wear either a short *chiton*, with a girdle at the waist and a scalloped turn-over edge at the top, leaving the right shoulder bare, or a simple *himation* alone leaving the upper part of the body bare save for the fold over the left shoulder. Two of the men wear hats that look rather like coal-heavers', but the details are damaged. The women wear a long *chiton* and *himation*, and garlands on their heads. The *chiton* is supported by a twisted girdle under the breasts and is long enough completely to cover the feet; the *himation* is draped over the left shoulder and arm, and round the hips and legs. The women also wear numerous bangles on their wrists but not on the upper arm. The man in the centre is holding a metal tankard of a type that is still familiar in Kashmīr and the North-West Frontier. The goblets held by the others are of a peculiarly distinctive shape, numerous specimens of which were found at Taxila in deposits dating from the Parthian period but not from any other period. Some were of earthenware, others of copper or bronze or silver. An example of the silver ones is shown in fig. 42. The characteristic features of these Parthian goblets are their carinated bodies, deeply flared mouths, horizontal flutings or bands, and disproportionately small bases, which were evidently meant to support them only when empty. Although a drinking-party, the men and women composing it make a sedate, dignified group very different from the boisterous orgy depicted on the toilet-tray, fig. 16.

Now let us go on to the next relief (fig. 41), which is in the British Museum. It is labelled 'Presentation of the bride to Siddhārtha', and that may well have been the label attached to it by the sculptor for the edification of the Buddhists. But, whatever the label, the scene portrayed is essentially the same as the drinking-scene of the previous panel, and the style, too, is identical. Indeed, so similar are the figures and faces of the men and women, their dress, ornaments, etc., even down to the scalloped borders of the men's tunics, that it is virtually certain they must have come from the same atelier. The only material difference between them is that in this relief two of the men are carrying bunches of lotuses in their hands and the three women nothing at all. What the men at the right and left ends have in their hands it is difficult to say, owing to mutilation of the stone. That at the left end looks suspiciously like a drinking vessel, but perhaps it is no more than a silver bowl with some 'wedding-cake' in it! But however this may be, it is clear that this slab marks a very early effort on the part of the Buddhists to give a religious complexion to a very mundane subject. Like the majority of sculptures of this period, the relief is made of chloritic mica-schist.

The next significant step is made apparent in the three following illustrations (figs. 43, 44, 45), in which the Greek setting is retained and the form and postures of the figures are Greek rather than local, but men and women alike are wearing local instead of Greek dress and all are carrying lotuses in their hands. The original provenance of these three panels is not known. Along with several other panels of the same kind they were formerly in the collection of the Church Missionary Society at Peshāwar. Figs. 43 and 44 are now in the Peshāwar Museum. The whereabouts of the other panel, said to be of yellowish-grey pot-stone, I have been unable to discover. In each panel there are six figures, three men and three women. All wear the native *dhoti*, tied with a girdle at the waist and reaching to the ankles. The upper part of the body is bare, except for a long shawl which is usually draped over the left shoulder and arm, and allowed to fall in a graceful fold below the right hip. Some of the women, however, wear the scarf draped over both shoulders, with a loose inflated length behind the head and shoulders, and the ends hanging down evenly on each side instead of both being on the left side. The men wear twisted turbans of the same kind as those worn by the stucco Bodhisattvas in Sirkap. The women wear wreaths above their carefully dressed coiffures. For ornaments, the men wear a necklace and a single bangle on each wrist; the women have a similar kind of necklace but several bangles on their wrists as well as heavy anklets on their ankles. Notwithstanding that the women are in native costume, it is noticeable that they are portrayed with small, firm breasts, not at all in the local tradition.

Framing the groups on each side is a Corinthian pilaster with rounded shaft and moulded base in a countersunk panel. The plinth below is enriched with a continuous moulding of Hellenistic pattern running round the whole structure. From the differing details of these mouldings and of the smaller mouldings below the pilasters it is evident that the three reliefs we are discussing belonged to separate structures. The Corinthian pilaster with rounded shaft is a constantly recurring feature of the panelled stūpa-reliefs of this and the succeeding period. Later on it tends to give place to the Corinthian pilaster with a flat shaft and usually more stunted proportions. On stūpas of the reign of Azes II in Sirkap both forms of pilaster were used side by side.

In the foregoing reliefs the lotuses in the hands of the men and women were sufficient to proclaim the Buddhist character of the monument, but in the case of other reliefs there is sometimes nothing at all to indicate a connexion with Buddhism. Thus, in Fig. 46 the six figures appear merely as fine, upstanding fighting men armed with swords and dressed in what is still a national costume on the North-West Frontier. Three of them are bearded and three beardless. Two of the beardless ones have their right hands raised with two fingers extended to signify Good Luck. All wear loose, baggy trousers tied at the ankles, with loosely fitting long-sleeved tunics. The figure at the right end has the sleeves pulled up, leaving the forearms bare; the one at the left end has his right sleeve hanging down, thus hiding the hand from view. In the cold hills of the Frontier such sleeves are serviceable for keeping the hands warm, and are still a common feature of Pathān dress. On their heads the men wear a close-fitting cap with side lapels and ribands hanging in front of the ears. The long, sheathed broadsword is suspended on a cord which passes over the left shoulder and across the back and front of the body above the waist line. The sword seems to resemble the long double-edged weapons found in Sirkap and the *spatha* of Roman auxiliaries in the East (*Taxila*, vol. II, pp. 544–5 and nos. 56–8). Framing the slab on either side is a Corinthian pilaster with rounded shaft in countersunk panel. The continuous base moulding of double torus section is similar to that of fig. 45, which possibly belonged to the same monument—a matter that could probably be decided by comparing their dimensions and the stones of which they are made, neither of which I have been able to ascertain. Let me add that the slab illustrated in fig. 46 used to be in the possession of the Church Missionary Society at Peshāwar; it is now in the Peshāwar Museum.

Another relief appertaining to the same group which shows no apparent connexion with Buddhism is the well-known one in the British Museum (fig. 47) of the Sea or River deities. There are six of them posed in a row between Corinthian pilasters: all splendidly athletic looking figures, wearing high boots and girt round the middle with acanthus leaves, which appear as if growing out of the body itself. All six are moustached and bearded and have long hair taken back from the forehead, with a small V-shaped device in front. To symbolize their connexion with the waters, each carries a broad-bladed boat paddle such as one can still see in use in Kashmīr, five holding it aloft on the left shoulder and the sixth leaning on it under his right arm. While the above features are common to all six deities, there is one point in which they show a very significant difference. For one only of the six has a normal male body from the hips upwards; the other five are provided with eight female breasts arranged in two lines above the navel, and the navel itself is much exaggerated in size. Other noteworthy points are that three of the figures have their right hands raised with two fingers extended in the gesture of Good Luck, and that one of the figures is holding what has been described as a dolphin—yet another symbol of the waters. That the six figures are sea or river deities can hardly be questioned. The multiple breasts, symbolical of their fertilizing power, though an unusual attribute, are not without parallels. They are found on statues of the Ephesian Artemis and on one of Zeus Stratios of Labranda (see P. Foucart in *Mon. Piot*, XVIII, pp. 145–75), and Mme Bazin-Foucher has ingeniously suggested that the name 'Thamimasadas' by which Herodotus tells us the Scythian Poseidon was known, was a compound formed of θαμά, meaning numerous or frequent, and a Scythian equivalent of the Greek μαζός, a breast (see E. Bazin-Foucher, 'Le nom scythique de Poseidon', *B.E.F.E.O.*, XLIV, fasc. 1, pp. 13–20). Thus it is possible, and indeed likely, that the five many-breasted figures on this relief present us with the Scythian conception of this god—a conception that must have been familiar to the Śaka peoples in Gandhāra. But why, it may be asked, are five only of the six portrayed as many-breasted? The answer, I suggest, is that the five were meant to represent the five rivers of the Panjāb, with emphasis thus laid on the all-important part they played in fertilizing its wide plains from the Himalayas to the sea. The sixth figure may represent the sea itself to which they are tributary but which does not have the same fertilizing power, though it brings abounding wealth in other ways to the Land of the Five Rivers.

Linked with the foregoing relief are two triangular panels made, like it, of greenish chloritic stone and carved in precisely the same style with winged Tritons of the traditional Hellenistic type. One of these panels (fig. 48) is in the British Museum, the other in the Peshāwar Museum, to which it was presented by the Church Missionary Society. That all three pieces belonged to the same monument can hardly be doubted; that they came from the hand of the same sculptor seems from their technique and style more than probable. The position occupied by the two triangular panels was no doubt under a raking cornice at the side of the steps leading up to a small stūpa-base. Note that, in fig. 48, the hair of the Triton is treated in exactly the same way as in the preceding relief, with a tufted V-shaped device over the forehead and long tresses behind falling down the back of the neck. Note also the same high cheek-bones, the same shaped nose and the same highly arched eye-brow.

To return, however, to the drinking-scenes, which enjoyed a wide popularity under the Parthians and exerted an enduring influence on the subsequent Buddhist art of Gandhāra. To the examples of these scenes already given I feel constrained to add three more which seem to me particularly instructive. Two of them (figs. 49 and 50) come from Haḍḍa in Southern Afghānistān. Unlike any of the reliefs from Taxila or the Peshāwar Valley, they are made of a white calcareous limestone, which is somewhat softer and coarser than the chloritic and micaceous schist or than the steatite and does not permit of the same degree of delicacy in the carving.

Fig. 49 is in the Musée Guimet in Paris. The scene on it comprises five figures, namely, an elderly couple, a younger couple, and a small child, presumably a family group of three generations. The older man is holding a wine-bowl in his hands; the woman by his side carries an amphora in her left arm, while with her right hand she holds out a bunch of grapes to the child. The younger man is playing on what appears to be a tambourine, and keeping time with his left foot. His wife, beside him, is playing on a two-stringed mandoline. The older man wears a *himation* only, falling from the left shoulder and leaving the body bare. The younger one has a short, sleeved tunic tied with a girdle round the hips. The dress of the women consists of a long, sleeved *chiton* reaching from the neck to the feet, and over it a *himation* draped from the left shoulder and across the legs. The wine-bowl held by the elder man is distinguished by a scalloped turn-over rim and two vertical handles. The treatment of the men's hair in small, well-defined but rather rough masses is noteworthy. It calls to mind the hair of the two figures on a triangular slab of chloritic schist in the Calcutta Museum, which depicts a Gigantomachia and is of about the same age as the relief from Haḍḍa (cf. Foucher, *A.G.-B.G.* vol. I, p. 245, fig. 125). It should also be remarked that none of the figures, on this or the following panel, from Haḍḍa is wearing a garland.

Fig. 50, which is now in the Kābul Museum, originally carried two groups separated by a Persepolitan pilaster, but it has been broken and only one figure of the right-hand group has survived. The other closely resembles the family group of fig. 49, but there are some slight differences. Thus, both couples are engaged in drinking, but their positions are reversed, the younger couple being on the left, the child in the middle, and the elder couple on the right. Instead of a tunic, the younger man has a *himation*, which his wife is holding open so as to leave his body exposed to view. There is a difference, too, in the dress of his wife, who is wearing a long double tunic instead of a tunic and *himation*. The hair of both men and women is treated in the same way as on the other relief, and the wine-bowls in the hands of the women are similar to the one held by the elder man in the other group. In point of style, design and execution the two reliefs are as characteristically Hellenistic as they are in their subject matter.

The last of the drinking-scenes that I have chosen for illustration (fig. 51) is carved on a lion-footed pedestal of dark micaceous schist now in the Lahore Museum. The distinctive pose of the two women, with their exposed backs and buttocks, resembles that of the women on the toilet-trays, figs. 16 to 18, and leaves no room for doubt that the pedestal belongs to the same period. We should observe, however, that in this case the women have been easternized to the extent of being provided with anklets and cross-straps on their backs. Round his forehead the elder man wears an ornamental band or *taenia* (the younger man's head is damaged).

Finally, and as a tail-piece to this chapter, I append a particularly fine statue of a crouching Atlant in the Lahore Museum (fig. 52). Such Atlants are familiar at all periods in Gandhāra art and afford, as we shall see, an instructive series of pointers for its history (see figs. 108, 145 and 146). This example, made of the same stone and approximately of the same age as fig. 51, is one of the oldest. It is a bold, masterly figure, with narrow waist and powerfully developed chest and limbs, and rather crudely modelled wings. The leafy wreath twined in the hair points to the influence of the Dionysus-Silenus cult.

## CHAPTER 6

# ADOLESCENCE

(FIGS. 53–68)

The influx of Hellenistic art described in the preceding chapter was short-lived. It began soon after the Parthian conquest of Gandhāra in *circa* A.D. 25, and ended abruptly with the advent of the Kushāns soon after A.D. 60. But it left an enduring mark on the nascent School of Buddhist sculpture, and its influence can be seen, clear and unmistakable, long after that date. This period, covered by the first four or five decades of Kushān rule, is in some ways the most fascinating in the history of the School. It is the period when Gandhāra art was in a formative, adolescent stage; when we can discern more clearly than at other times the efforts of the artists to overcome their initial difficulties, to reconcile Greek and local ideas, and to create from them a new synthesis of religious art suited to the needs of the Buddhist Church. Of all the sculptures dating from this period some of the earliest and most attractive are comprised in the collection which formerly belonged to the Guides' Mess at Mardān. For the preservation of these sculptures we owe no small debt to the officers of the Guides; but it could be wished that they had spared themselves the trouble of trying to brighten up the sculptures by occasionally blacking and polishing them, since the effect has been completely to obscure the surface texture and fine finish, and to make it virtually impossible to secure satisfactory photographs. How disastrous for reproduction this maltreatment has proved can be seen by comparing fig. 56, which was taken in 1927, with fig. 54, which was taken more than half a century ago when the relief was first unearthed. I stress this point the more because many of the other illustrations which follow suffer from the same serious defect, and it is important that full allowance should be made for it, if the merits of the sculptures are to be correctly assessed.

I have labelled this group of sculptures the 'Mardān' group for no other reason than that they happened to be preserved in that place, before being transferred to the Peshāwar Museum where they are now. Of their original provenance no reliable record seems to have been kept. From inquiries I made on the spot in 1903 I concluded that the majority had come from Swāt, but there were some that had come from other sites, and it would, therefore, be misleading to call it the Swāt group.

With these prefatory remarks I now turn to some characteristic examples. The first of these to merit our notice is fig. 53—a small, unpretentious slab about 8 in. high. The six figures disposed in a single row are closely akin to those on several of the slabs discussed in the last chapter (e.g. figs. 40 and 41) and are clearly carrying on the Hellenistic tradition. Hellenistic, too, are their poses and the treatment of their drapery, with its graceful folds and careful definition. Unfortunately, this is one of the many sculptures that have been blackened and polished, so that the photograph gives little idea of the delicate workmanship. The scene portrayed has been identified by M. Foucher (*A.G.-B.G.* vol. I, p. 474, fig. 239) as the Presentation of the Jetavana Garden at Śrāvastī. Towards the left end of the relief stands the Buddha, distinguished by his halo, with a companion monk behind him. In front of the Buddha is the merchant Anāthapiṇḍada, with a water-vessel in his hand to symbolize the gift he is making, and behind him three more lay-worshippers, one of whom is holding a small object in his hand—possibly a bowl of coins for the purchase of the land. Assuming that M. Foucher is right, and I see no reason to doubt it, this relief affords a striking illustration of the wide gulf between Gandhāra and Indian art. The stock Indian version is much more realistic (*loc. cit.* p. 475, fig. 240). It shows us the Jetavana Garden with the Buddha (represented by his tree), Anāthapiṇḍada in front of him with a libation vessel in his hand, attendants engaged in covering the ground with coins, and even the bullock-cart which brought the coins and the two bullocks outspanned beside it. Compared with this, the Gandhāra version is dull and unimaginative, but it has the advantage of dignity and repose, qualities which in the long run were more suited to the development of a great and far-reaching ecclesiastical art.

In the history of the Gandhāra School this relief has a unique value. *It is the earliest representation of the Buddha by a Gandhāra artist known to us.* We are in fact here present at the birth, or as near the birth as it is possible to be, of the canonical Buddha standing image which was now to replace the older symbolism of the church and to become for future generations of Buddhists the centre and focus of their liturgical worship.

Therefore it is of supreme interest to observe that in this relief the Buddha is of the same stature and appearance as the rest of the figures, with nothing yet evident to distinguish him from the monk beside him except his halo. Whether the Buddha was at this stage crowned with the familiar top-knot (*ushṇīsha*) is a point that the damaged state of the relief prevents our determining. Within a few years of the carving of this relief the *ushṇīsha* was to become an invariable feature of all Buddha images, and it is at least highly probable that it was present in this one,[1] but we are not yet entitled to take it for granted. The halo, it need hardly be said, was a Greek invention; and the monk's dress worn by the Buddha and his companion was also Greek: of a pattern which, as M. Foucher long ago pointed out, is exemplified in the well-known Sophocles statue in the Lateran Museum. Presumably the dress had been adopted by the Buddhist *bhikshus* at a time when Greek fashions were prevalent in that area. It is a type of dress that is not found among the early figural reliefs of India.

One other characteristic of this relief that deserves particular notice is the fact that all six figures have the same distinctive cast of countenance: the same refined and slightly pointed nose, the same small drooping moustache, the same strongly marked cheek-bones. These are features that we shall encounter again in other sculptures.

Closely linked in age and style with the foregoing are the two reliefs illustrated in figs. 54 and 55, the one depicting the 'Interpretation of Māyā's dream', the other the 'Seven Steps of the Infant Buddha'. The two panels came from the same monument in Swāt, where these two small but excellent photographs were taken by Mr Caddy sometime before the panels passed into the possession of the Guides. By the side of fig. 54, fig. 56 makes it all too clear that the first of the two panels has suffered much from blacking and polishing before this later photo (fig. 56) was taken. In the same way fig. 57 shows how much the other panel had suffered from mutilation, particularly to the infant Buddha's legs.

In the scene of the Dream Interpretation King Śuddhodana is seated, full-face, on a richly decorated throne, on the back of which lean two women attendants with fly-whisks in their hands. Above the king's head is the royal umbrella fringed with bells. To his left and right, seated on

[1] [A more recent photograph of the relief reproduced in fig. 53 shows that, as was surmised by the author, the *ushṇīsha* is indeed present. See I. Lyons and H. Ingholt, *Gandhāran Art in Pakistan*, New York, 1957, fig. 95. ED.]

wicker stools, are the Rishi Asita and his nephew Naradatta. Both are holding water vessels in their left hands. Māyā, who is usually present in later versions of this scene is absent from this one.

In the companion piece depicting the 'Seven Steps' the infant Buddha stands under the royal umbrella in the centre, and behind him is an attendant holding the umbrella shaft with his left hand and a fly-whisk in his right. On the infant's left is Indra, recognizable by his head-dress and thunderbolt (*vajra*), and on his right, Brahmā, with the Brāhman's *kamaṇḍalu* in his left hand. Behind the two gods were six other heavenly beings, three on one side and three on the other.

Excluding their borders these two panels are less than 6 in. high and of exquisitely fine workmanship, with the quality of ivory miniatures rather than stone carvings. Their close affinity with the Partho-Greek reliefs described in the last chapter is evident in many features: in the formal, scenic character of the composition and the self-conscious poses of the individual figures; in the careful delineation of the facial features notwithstanding their minute scale; in the graceful draping of the robes and masterly precision in the modelling of their folds; and in the framing of the panels between pairs of rounded Corinthian pilasters. These and other details of style and technique make it clear beyond question that these two panels follow at no long interval in the track of the Partho-Greek reliefs, and this conclusion is confirmed by the relationship in which they stand to later members of the same group which we shall presently examine. On the other hand, there is a radical difference between these panels and their Partho-Greek predecessors. The latter, as we have seen, were little more than servile imitations of Hellenistic originals, with the actors sometimes dressed in local instead of Greek costume, sometimes carrying a lotus instead of a wine-cup in their hands, to give a Buddhist atmosphere to the scene. But the changes are superficial and do not affect their essentially Hellenistic character. Here, in these two panels, it is different. The sculptor still has the Greek outlook, is still inspired by Greek ideals, still employs the Greek technique and expresses himself in the Greek idiom. But he is now moving in a new atmosphere, the religious atmosphere of Buddhism, is deeply immersed in its sacred traditions and is putting all his skill and artistry into the narration of its legends. Reliefs of this character are manifestly too mature and complex to have been created overnight or by the genius of a single artist. They presuppose earlier efforts of a more empirical, less assured kind, and it may be hoped that examples of these may one day be turned up by the spade of the excavator. Meanwhile we must be content to recognize that, with these panels, we are now for the first time coming face to face with the real Graeco-Buddhist Art of Gandhāra—an art which was dependent for its life-blood as much on the traditions and inspiration of Buddhism as on those of the local Hellenism, and which could have been born nowhere else in Asia but on the soil of Gandhāra.

Before taking leave of these reliefs there are two more features that we ought to notice. One is that the Corinthian pilasters are no longer such an integral part of the architectural design as they were in the preceding group (figs. 43–47). In that group the pilasters were supported on a continuous moulded plinth, which had the effect of linking them and the carved panels between them in a common scheme of decoration. In the later panels the continuous moulded plinth is lacking, the pilaster bases being carried to the bottom of the panel, with a plain flat band to support the reliefs between. It is a small point but it marks a definite change in the architectural integration of the design.

The second feature is the fine surface decoration carved in low relief on the throne and footstool of fig. 54. In spite of its being on such a small scale the details of the patterns, of which the 'rosette and sheaf' is the principal, are remarkably clear and effective. It is only at this period, so far as I know, that this highly refined type of ornamentation is found.

The next relief is slightly larger than the foregoing, being about 10·5 in. in height, including the plinth (fig. 58). The stone of which it is made is said to be a dark micaceous schist, whether chloritic could not be determined owing to the black pigment covering the surface. The scene portrayed is the 'Bath of the infant Buddha'. In the foreground two female attendants are supporting the child on a three-legged stool, while Indra and Brahmā pour water from *lotas* over his head. To right and left, four more figures, doubtless divine, have come to adore the new-born Buddha. Behind the infant's head is the usual halo; above, the usual umbrella. The likeness of this to the two preceding reliefs is obvious. There is the same facial expression, the same short and delicately modelled nose, the same bone structure of the cheeks, the same draping of the robes, the same framing of the panel between Corinthian pilasters. But the workmanship in this relief is not up to the same high standard. The modelling of the attendant figures is heavier, the folds of their draperies coarser. Indeed, in the case of one of the kneeling women, the folds, instead of being modelled, are indicated merely by incised, wavering lines. This may mean nothing more than that the carving at this point was unfinished, but, quite apart from this particular defect, we cannot fail to be conscious of the incipient signs of failing technical skill visible in this relief.

Fig. 59, the following piece, is exceptionally interesting. It is a fragment of chloritized micaceous schist which came from Loriyān Tangai and is now in the Calcutta Museum. No doubt it represents the First Sermon (cf. figs. 4 and 117). In the centre is the Buddha, represented by a pillar surmounted by three interlaced wheels symbolizing at once the Law (*dharmacakra*) and the Trinity or Three Jewels (*triratna*). The triple wheels are supported by a *yaksha* emerging *à mi-corps* from the foliate capital of the Corinthian pillar, on the shaft of which is a vine-scroll in low relief, with the footprints of the Teacher on the base below. To the right and left of the pillar are two arched doorways, and in front of each, in attitudes of worship, are two shaven monks representing Kauṇḍinya and his companions, one of whom is missing where the stone is broken at the left-hand bottom corner. On the left side of the fragment are three celestials, come to adore the Buddha, and above them a winged angel holding an offering in his left hand. The flat base of the panel is enriched with a band of rosette-and-sheaf pattern. In the details of this relief there is much to merit attention. We note in particular the similarity of the fine surface ornament, including the rosette-and-sheaf pattern, to that on the throne of Śuddhodana in fig. 54, and also the similarity of the fine delineation of the monks' features. On the other hand, we cannot help being struck by the deterioration in the treatment of the robes, with little more than incised lines to represent their folds, just as in the decadent Graeco-Śaka work of an earlier generation. But while this panel evidences a further stage in the decline of technical skill, it also evidences a brave effort on the part of the sculptor to introduce a touch of realism and variety into the scene by depicting the monks as if they had just emerged from the doorway of their cells. It matters little that his experiment was not very successful: that the doorways are oddly awry. It was a step in the right direction—a step that was eventually to lead to a freer and more decorative kind of composition, though to the end, let it be said, Gandhāra art never succeeded in attaining anything like the freedom of the Early Indian School.

If further confirmation of the date of this fragment is needed, it is furnished by three of the celestial beings at the left side of the fragment. One of these is the winged angel at the top. In sculptures of the Early Indian School winged angels are the rule rather than the exception, but in the Gandhāra School they are very rare, and are found, so far as I know, only in work of this early period. The second is the *deva* with drooping moustache and twisted turban, standing immediately below the angel. He bears a quite remarkable likeness to a figure of chloritized micaceous schist which I unearthed at the Dharmarājikā at Taxila in 1913 (fig. 60). Such a striking similarity makes it impossible to doubt that both pieces came from the same atelier, if not from the hand of the same sculptor. The third is the lowest one of the *deva* figures with a brush instead of a drooping moustache. Celestial beings with this particular kind of moustache were one of the stock types in the early art of Gandhāra, but the type does not seem to have survived for more than two or three generations.

To return, however, to the sculptures from the Guides' Mess. The next in chronological sequence are two panels belonging to the same stūpa (figs. 61 and 62). The first depicts the grass-cutter Svastika presenting a bundle of grass to the Bodhisattva on his way to the bodhi tree. The second depicts the adoration of the Bodhisattva's head-dress in the Trayastriṁśa Heaven. These two panels doubtless issued from the same atelier. Their close affinity to the sculptures already described is obvious. Compare, for example, the attendant worshippers in fig. 62 with those in the Bath Scene, fig. 58. The stylistic resemblance speaks for itself. But the carving is steadily becoming coarser, and losing little by little the sensitiveness of the earlier work; most of the actors, too, are of heavier, more thick-set, build. On the other hand, the artists' outlook continues to expand, their ideas to multiply, their work to become more eloquent. The representation of the Buddha in bodily form simplifies and encourages the portrayal of scenes from his daily life, which from now onwards become more numerous and diversified. From the start there seems to have been some confusion about the figures of the Buddha and the Bodhisattva, but this is a detail which mattered little so long as the meaning of the scene was clear. What did matter was that the Buddha was emerging at this time in a form that could instantly be recognized. In the case of fig. 53 we were left in some doubt as to whether the Buddha, then appearing for the first time, was distinguished by his *ushṇīsha* or not.[1] In this, his next, appearance, there is no such doubt. The *ushṇīsha* is larger and more conspicuous than in later sculptures and the halo is emphasized by a well-defined rim. These, with the Greek monastic robes, are characteristic traits shared by all the Buddha figures belonging to this group, and they are more than enough to make those figures instantly recognizable. Along with the Buddha, his inseparable companion, the Vajrapāṇi, also makes his appearance, and it is noteworthy that his characteristic dress at this period is identical in all respects with that worn by the attendant (?) in the Graeco-Parthian drinking-scenes (figs. 40, 41), namely, a short *chiton* or tunic, caught in round the waist and provided with a scalloped turn-over edge at the top. Another point for passing notice is that some of the *devas* in fig. 62 wear the same long, unconfined locks as the youthful Brahmā in fig. 58 but with the addition of a small top-knot. To the above examples I have added fig. 63, a panel in the Berlin Museum, because of its outstanding clarity and close resemblance to them. A feature of this fine panel is the care with which the pupils of the eyes are delineated. As to the outsize *ushṇīsha*, see above, fig. 61. The stūpa which yielded the above panels seems also to have yielded several small pilasters which served to divide the panels one from another. At this period such pilasters usually took the form of Corinthian half-columns with rounded shafts. Here the half-column is replaced by a female figure standing on a vase pedestal of Persepolitan pattern under a canopy of foliage. Two examples are illustrated in figs. 64 and 65. The first is a female guard in native dress, armed with shield and spear. The second is a musician, in Greek dress, playing on a lute. The motif of a *yakshī* standing on a Persepolitan vase base is a familiar one in the Early Indian School at Bodh-Gayā and elsewhere. The two pilasters are of the same height as the panels and are said to be of the same dark, micaceous schist.

From another stūpa of slightly later date come the two reliefs 66 and 67, each about 15 in. high and adorned with the same running pattern along its lower edge. Fig. 66 depicts the Buddha visiting a Brāhman

[1] [See note on p. 42. ED.]

ascetic in his hut; fig. 67 the attack of Māra. In the former panel the Buddha accompanied by his Vajrapāṇi, is standing at the entrance to the hut, within which the hermit is seated on his rolled-up mat. The Buddha here is almost an exact replica of the Buddha in fig. 61, with the same moustache, the same wide-open eyes, the same over-sized *ushṇīsha*, the same rimmed halo, and the same monk's dress, the only slight difference being that his outer robe (the Greek *himation*) is draped less stiffly over his left arm. The Vajrapāṇi, too, is wearing the same short tunic with the same scalloped border as in the other relief, but in this panel he is no longer a bearded man but a young Brahmacārin with the characteristic locks of the Brahmā in fig. 58. As to the Brāhman ascetic, the modelling of his features is rather more sensitive than that of the other figures, and we are reminded that the motif of a Brāhman ascetic seated at the entrance of his hut was sufficiently topical in the first century to be engraved on a copper seal as a canting badge of a certain Brahmadatta.[1] It may be, therefore, that the sculptor of this panel was more at home with this particular figure than with the others.

The companion panel, fig. 67, shows a precisely similar Buddha seated on his grass-strewn throne beneath a canopy of leaves. He is in the Earth-touching attitude (*bhūmi-sparśa-mudrā*). On his left is Māra, sword in hand, being held in check by Indra; on his right, one of Māra's warriors, similarly held by Brahmā. In front of the throne are two more fallen warriors, and above, two pairs of angels bringing offerings to the Buddha. The figure of Brahmā resembles the youthful Brahmā in fig. 58 and bears a striking likeness to the Vajrapāṇi in fig. 66, but is not wearing the short Greek *chiton* which distinguished the Vajrapāṇi figures at this period. His long-sleeved coat seems to be of the same pattern as that worn by Indra. In our examination of these panels we must not forget that at the time they were executed Gandhāra Buddhist sculpture was still in the making, and we must not be surprised to find occasional anomalies and inconsistencies. For example, in fig. 66 the artist did not stop to ask himself whether it was before or after his Enlightenment that the Buddha visited the hermit. Whatever the occasion, it was enough for him to repeat the accepted type of the Teacher, complete with *ūrṇā*, *ushṇīsha* and halo. Similarly, in regard to 67, it is fruitless to argue that

[1] Cf. *Taxila*, vol. I, pp. 170–1; vol. II, p. 680, no. 24; vol. III, pl. 208, no. 50; *ibid.* vol. II, pp. 720–1, no. 134; vol. III, pl. 222, no. 134.

the tree canopying the Buddha ought to be a pipal, or that Indra is wearing the wrong sort of head-dress. In the eyes of the artist the *śāla* tree, invariably present in the familiar Nirvāṇa scenes, was the tree *par excellence* associated with the Buddha and he used this tree as a convenient cliché, whether he was telling the story of the Buddha's Enlightenment or his Death, or of his meetings with the hermit or the grass-cutter. As to Indra's dress the artist has evidently indulged his imagination in clothing the god in the local kind of pyjama-like trousers. For his head-dress there is some authority, since the lower part of it at least is paralleled in the Indra of fig. 84. But we must not be too punctilious about such details. After all, artists who could make edifying pictures for the Buddhists out of Graeco-Parthian drinking-parties were not likely to bother their heads overmuch about the difference between a *ficus religiosa* and a *shorea robusta* tree or about the particular fashion in toques favoured by Indra.

Of the many *parinirvāṇa* scenes known to me the oldest, I think, is one from the Guides' Mess Collection which is reproduced in fig. 68, but this photograph does not, unfortunately, show the entire panel, which comprises the remnant of a Corinthian pilaster on the left and the mutilated figure of a monk at the foot of the couch on the right. In the centre of the panel is the dead Buddha on a couch. In front, the mourning monks. At the head, the Vajrapāṇi. At the foot, the newly arrived Mahākāśyapa (not in the photo). Behind the couch, two weeping Malla chieftains with another monk (?) on their right and a representative *deva* of the stock type on their left. To complete the scene, two *śāla* trees are added in the background with dryads or tree-spirits ensconced among their foliage. In this composition—the earliest that has survived but by no means the first of its kind—there is much to engage our attention. First there is the poignant sorrow written in the faces and actions of the mourners. The Malla chiefs are unrestrained in their grief; the monks, as is fitting, are more resigned; and so, too, is the Vajrapāṇi; but tears, which the sculptor has been at pains to show, are streaming down their cheeks. Only the *deva* stands tearless and reverently saluting the dead; for it is against the nature of a god to weep or display strong emotion. Then, we note the care with which the artist has delineated the faces of the mourners, distinguishing between those of the monks and Vajrapāṇi on the one hand, and of the wild, uncouth-looking Mallas on the other, with the *deva* in a class by himself. As to the recumbent figure of the Buddha himself, the artist has made a brave effort to disclose the lines of his form beneath the folds of the monk's robe, and to make it appear as if the dead were sleeping relaxed and peaceful on his side. In this respect there is a striking difference between this relief and later versions of the same scene in which the Buddha is made to appear like a full-length image of stone laid, stiff and rigid, on its side. Finally, we note that in this panel the Vajrapāṇi, clad in the orthodox tunic of the period and only a little less sturdy and thick-set than in the earlier reliefs, is standing at the head of the couch, whereas in later versions he is usually placed on another side (cf. figs. 72, 87, 127–9 below).

CHAPTER 7

# ADOLESCENCE (CONTINUED)

(FIGS. 69–86)

## (a) THE SANGHAO-NATHU GROUP

The sculptures of the Mardān group described in the preceding chapter represent the main stream of Gandhāra art during its adolescence. Besides these there are other contemporary groups which, though of a more provincial character, nevertheless contributed materially to the development of that art. One such group was centred in the hilly country around Sanghao, Nathu, and Miyān Khān on the north-west border of Buner. Another is known to us chiefly from the reliefs of the well-known stūpa at Sikri some ten miles north of Shāhbāz-Garhī; others from miscellaneous sculptures whose provenance is often uncertain. These various groups came into being in different places and at different times, and each had its own traditions, its own style, its own technique. We must be careful, therefore, how we make use of particular features, whether stylistic, technical or iconographic, as criteria of date, since it is manifest that such features could seldom have made their appearance simultaneously in different groups.

Of the minor groups named above, the Sanghao-Nathu group is represented by a variety of sculptures, some belonging to the adolescent stage, others to the periods of maturity or decline. Of the adolescent ones I have chosen four typical examples for illustration (figs. 69–72). The stone of which they are made is said to be greyish-white micaceous schist, but my information on this point needs verification. Each of the four slabs seems to have come from a different structure, though there is a close affinity in style and workmanship between figs. 69 and 70 on the one hand and figs. 71 and 72 on the other.

Fig. 69, which is in the Bombay Museum, depicts the submission of the Nāga Apalāla. Though the workmanship is rough, the story is told simply and effectively—more effectively, I think, than in some of the later and more sophisticated versions. To the left, in the foreground, are the Nāga-rāja and his wife, emerging from the waters of a tank. Above them, among the rocks, is a dwarf-like *yaksha*, smiting the mountain with a *vajra* and making the earth tremble. On the right is the figure of the Buddha in a protective pose, and behind him the Vajrapāṇi, here clad in a monk's robe like the Master himself, while above him, in the background, appear the head and shoulders of another monk. On the forehead of the Vajrapāṇi is a curious mark, which appears to be a third eye, suggesting an Indian origin. This Vajrapāṇi beside the Buddha is quite distinct from the *yaksha* engaged in smiting the mountain side. The fact that the latter has a *vajra* in his hand does not make a Vajrapāṇi of him. Primarily the *vajra* or thunderbolt was an attribute of Indra, as, from time immemorial, it had been of the Greek Zeus. But, as the weapon *par excellence* of irresistible force, it was put into the hands of other deities or superhuman beings, of Athene and Poseidon, for example, among the Greeks; of the Vajrapāṇi and of this earth-shaking *yaksha* among the Buddhists.

A feature of the Sanghao-Nathu reliefs is the obvious difficulty which the artists experienced over the modelling of the eyes. The common practice, well illustrated in figs. 69 and 70, was to make the eye-balls unnaturally large and protruding, like those of people afflicted with exophthalmic goitre. But in some cases, as in the Buddha of fig. 71, the sculptor hardly attempted to carve the eye-balls at all. Doubtless this very amateurish use of the chisel was due to the same lack of technical experience as the wide-open staring eyes which characterized the Graeco-Śaka sculptures of an earlier date, but the resulting treatment of the eyes differed in the two cases and there is no reason to assume any direct connexion between them.

Another notable feature of these reliefs, well exemplified in fig. 69, is the treatment of the drapery. Admittedly the workmanship is rough and perfunctory, and the standard is incomparably below that of the Partho-Hellenistic work of an older generation, but the artist does not content himself, except very rarely, with merely indicating the folds by a series of incised lines such as we have observed in some of the other groups. He models them boldly and not ungracefully, in such a way as to bring out their substance and depth or, in technical phraseology, their tri-dimensional effect.

Fig. 70, representing the Worship of the Three Jewels, or, possibly, the First Sermon, is a very dull and uninspired composition compared with fig. 59. The design of the *triratna* and the grouping of the adoring monks exhibit none of the imagination or inventive effort visible in the Loriyān Tangai fragment. Indeed, the only feature in which this relief shows to advantage is the treatment of the monks' robes, which, though rough and summary, shows a more realistic and correct sense for plastic form.

Fig. 71 depicts Gautama with two Brāhman ascetics. The subject recalls fig. 66, but in this panel, in spite of obvious shortcomings, the scene is altogether more developed and expressive. Here the aged Brāhman, a spare, emaciated figure, is sitting at the side of a hut, which faces front instead of the usual sideways, and inside of which his companion is seated in deep thought, in an attitude which reminds us of Rodin's 'Le penseur'. Though the execution is rough and sketchy, I regard this figure as exceptionally telling. The other figures, on the right of the panel, are less successful. Gautama himself is facing front, without any apparent concern in the Brāhman by his side; and his attendant Vajrapāṇi, who here takes the form of a Brahmacārin, is hardly less detached. Apart from the general character of this relief there are a few minor details worth noting. One is the unusually youthful appearance of the Buddha, which would be wholly appropriate to him at the time when this particular episode took place. And, indeed, it is possible that the artist had this fact in mind. On the other hand, it is noteworthy that the Buddha is just as youthful on his death-bed in fig. 72, and it looks therefore as if this may have been a stock type of the Buddha in the particular atelier from which this relief emanated.

Another point worth noting is that, in contrast with the Buddha of fig. 69, the Buddha here is devoid of his usual halo. It is the same in the Nirvāṇa scene of fig. 72, but in the latter the omission might conceivably be due to the awkwardness of a halo when the head is resting on a pillow. Here, no such explanation is possible and we can only infer that the artist responsible for these reliefs did not regard the halo as indispensable.

Yet another small point is that the *deva*, if *deva* he is, at the right-hand top corner is provided with an *ushṇīsha* (or with a top-knot exactly resembling an *ushṇīsha*) on the crown of his head. I mention this detail only because a theory, quite unsubstantiated, has been advanced that figures with the *ushṇīsha* must be either the Buddha himself or a sort of spiritual double of the Buddha, which this adoring figure clearly is not.

Finally, it should be observed that the Corinthian pilaster on the right of this panel has a flat shaft instead of the rounded one more familiar at this time, and that the face of the shaft is relieved with the roughly drawn figure of a monk. From remains unearthed in the city of Sirkap at Taxila we know that as far back as the reign of Azes II, that is, the beginning of the Christian era, the same stūpas were adorned with both types of Corinthian pilasters—the rounded and the flat, and there was no reason why one more than another of these types should subsequently have been preferred by the sculptors of Gandhāra. It is a fact, however, and a rather surprising one, that the rounded type is commonly found in the earlier reliefs, the flat one in the later. I say surprising, because a rounded shaft is so much more difficult to carve than a flat one. In the case of the Sanghao-Nathu group, however, the flat type seems to have been preferred from the outset, or at least as far back as we can trace the history of this group. Possibly it was to the influence of this group that the flat type subsequently owed its widespread popularity.

The death of the Buddha (fig. 72) was one of the earliest and most familiar subjects of Gandhāra art. One version of it we have already discussed (fig. 68); others we shall discuss in later chapters (figs. 87, 127–9). In all of them the essential elements were well established by tradition and unalterable, namely, the Buddha stretched at full length on his couch, the Vajrapāṇi, the sorrowing monks, the *devas*, the *śāla* trees in the background, and frequently but not invariably the Malla chiefs. But in the treatment of the individual figures and their grouping there was plenty of scope for the imagination and skill of the artist. Thus, if we compare this relief from the Lower monastery at Nathu with fig. 68, we observe several significant differences. Here, the form of the Buddha is somewhat more rigid, though not so rigid and statuesque as in later versions; the Vajrapāṇi here is standing at the further side of the couch instead of at its head, with three *devas* (?) on his right, three monks on his left, while Ananda, who has collapsed in front of the couch, is being helped to his feet by a brother *bhikshu* at the head of the couch. In this relief, too, the Malla chiefs are omitted; and so, also, are the dryads of the *śāla* trees. Of the three figures on the right of the Vajrapāṇi, Brahmā is recognizable in the figure with flowing locks at the edge of the panel, and the one next to him is presumably Indra though there is nothing special by which to identify him. But what of the charming young figure between the latter and the Vajrapāṇi? His strange head-covering looks in the photo like a canopy of snake hoods, but I must leave it to someone else to examine the original and decide whether he is a Nāga-rāja or not. For other figures in this relief, the reader may consult Foucher, *A.G.-B.G.*, vol. I, p. 565 and fig. 281.

From what has been said above it will be apparent that there is something strangely anomalous about the art of this Sanghao-Nathu School. On the one hand, the workmanship, that is, the actual carving of the stone, is for the most part coarse and unskilful—so much so that one might conclude from it that the School had but recently come into being when these sculptures were executed. On the other hand, the technique of the relief-work, the modelling of individual figures and the handling of the group compositions—all demonstrate a stage of development far removed from the primitive. And the orthodox way in which the sacred legends are set forth also goes to show that the School already had well-established traditions behind it. Although, therefore, these sculptures happen to be the earliest examples of this group known to us, it is clear that they must have been preceded by many still earlier efforts going back to the early part of the first century A.D.

All things considered, I incline to assign these panels to the latter part of the Adolescent Period, i.e. to the last quarter of the first century A.D. In the next chapter we shall encounter some further examples of the Sanghao-Nathu School, which illustrate its art in a more mature form (figs. 87–89 and 91).

### (*b*) THE SIKRI GROUP

Most of the sculptures belonging to this group come from the small site of Sikri, and chiefly from a single stūpa whose remains are now in the Lahore Museum. It seems likely, therefore, that they may have been the work of an atelier situated somewhere in the neighbourhood of Shāhbāz-Garhī. Though of relatively little artistic merit, the sculptures furnish valuable data both for the history of Gandhāra art and for Buddhist iconography. Their style, generally, is prosaic, the figures formal and stilted, the composition uninspired. But the quality of the carvings is not uniform. In some panels the figures are not without a measure of grace and comeliness; in others they are ungainly and even ugly. In some, the folds of the draperies are modelled with a correct appreciation of form and substance; in others they are sketchily indicated by incised lines. These and other differences of design and workmanship were manifestly due to the varying abilities of the sculptors engaged on the decoration of this monument, and must not be taken as evidence of any differences in the age of the reliefs.

Various features of the Sikri carvings combine to show that they cannot be far removed in date from those already described in this and the preceding chapter. Prominent among such features are the Corinthian pilasters with rounded shafts set in countersunk panels, the ungainly-looking figures of the Buddha with their outsize and frequently rimmed haloes, and the presence of *śāla* trees in scenes with which they have no legendary connexion. Taken together these features are a significant index to the approximate age of the carvings and justify their inclusion in the Adolescent Period. On the other hand, there are other and no less significant features which point to a somewhat later date than that to which we have assigned the Mardān and Sanghao-Nathu groups. Thus, the youthful Vajrapāṇi of figs. 75 and 76 is a type that we have so far not met with but with which we shall become familiar in the period of Maturity. Similarly, the heavy canopy of pipal leaves over the head of the Buddha in fig. 77 is an outstanding characteristic of certain reliefs of this class dating from the early years of the Mature period. And the neat, trim figures of the *devas*, with their carefully tailored costumes and schematic grouping, point to the deepening influence of Early Indian art and the development of the Mature style in Gandhāra which resulted from it. Taking everything into consideration, I think that we shall not be far wrong if we place the Sikri carvings near the end of the first century A.D., where they mark at once the close of the Adolescent Period of Gandhāra art and the advent of its maturity.

The panels which adorn the circular base of the Sikri Stūpa are thirteen in number, and carved from the same stone as the rest of its facing—a dark grey, almost black, carbonaceous schist. Of the five selected for illustration, fig. 73 depicts the Dipaṅkara Jātaka. It is the first version of this familiar story that we have encountered, but we shall encounter others later. Here we see the Dipaṅkara Buddha as much the same ungainly figure as the Gautama Buddha was in the Mardān and Sanghao-Nathu reliefs, with the same robes, the same *ushṇīsha*, and the same expansive halo. The only difference is that in the intervening years his stature has grown a little taller in proportion to the people around him, and his *ushṇīsha* a little smaller. We also observe that, in this relief, he is attended, not by the usual Vajrapāṇi, but by a *bhikshu*. In later versions of this scene, however, he has his own Vajrapāṇi. In front of the Dipaṅkara the young Sumati (or Sumedha) is repeated four times: first bargaining with the flower-seller in the gateway of the city, then throwing his lotus flowers in the air, then prostrating himself at the feet of the Master, and lastly suspended like the lotus flowers in the air. Two minor points in this carving that are worth noting are the small cut made in the arris of the base for the foot of Sumati (a very unusual device), and the heavy wreath worn by the flower-seller—a survival from the Graeco-Parthian period.

Fig. 74 portrays the Bodhisattva in the Tushita heaven, deliberating on his impending earthly birth, a suggestion of which is provided by his lotus throne. His attire is similar to that of the trim-looking gods beside him. The celestial beings above the heads of the Tushita gods are distinguished by a simpler dress, *ushṇīsha* and halo. In other panels of this stūpa some of the *devas* wear jewelled head-dresses and ornaments, but in every case they are provided with a halo. In reliefs of the Early Indian School such celestial beings usually appear floating like birds in the air, and it is thus that they are occasionally depicted by the sculptors of Gandhāra. But the more usual practice in Gandhāra is to portray them at full length in a standing posture, with their lower limbs hidden behind the heads and shoulders of the figures below them, thus avoiding the incongruous appearance of one row of figures standing on the heads of another. At Sikri, most of the reliefs, including the one we are discussing, are marred by this patent defect, but fig. 76 is a notable exception to the general rule.

In fig. 75 the Buddha is listening to the prophecy of the Nāga king Kālika and his queen. The composition is formal and unimaginative but the workmanship is conscientious and refined, and the figures of the two Nāgas and of the *devas* above, who appear actually to be moving in flight through the air, are not lacking in grace and charm. Observe the conventional *śāla* trees in the background and the youthful brahmacārin-type of Vajrapāṇi—a type destined to become familiar in later sculpture.

Compared with the preceding panel fig. 76 makes but a poor showing. It portrays the Bodhisattva in the act of receiving from the grass-cutter,

Svastika, a bundle of grass wherewith to strew his seat beneath the bodhi tree. In point of composition the group is much the same as its neighbours; the Vajrapāṇi behind the Buddha is of a similar type to the one in fig. 75, and the celestial *devas* also resemble those in other panels though, as already noted, they are disposed more convincingly. But the workmanship here is decidedly inferior, particularly in the handling of the draperies. Whereas in figs. 74 and 75, for example, the form and substance of the drapery folds are modelled realistically in the stone, here the modelling has been scamped, and the folds, for the most part, merely sketched in with the point of the chisel. Notice, too, the faulty drawing of the Bodhisattva's right hand and the perfunctory, wig-like treatment of the *deva*'s hair in the right-hand top corner, which calls to mind the decadent carving in some of the later Graeco-Śaka toilet-trays. In fairness to the sculptor of this relief, however, it should be added that the photograph of it reproduced in fig. 76 makes the workmanship appear worse than it really is.

The episode illustrated in fig. 77 is the presentation to the Buddha, immediately after his Enlightenment, of the four begging-bowls by the Regents of the Four Quarters. As set out by the artist, the scene is a very conventional and schematic one, but the workmanship is careful and competent. I have included this panel among my illustrations of the Sikri Stūpa chiefly because the figure of the seated Buddha beneath its heavy canopy of pipal leaves affords a specific link with a number of sculptures of this class which date from the beginning of the mature period of Gandhāra art (cf. figs. 100, 101), and thus corroborate the conclusion as to its date arrived at on stylistic and other grounds.

### (*c*) MISCELLANEOUS SCULPTURES OF THE ADOLESCENT PERIOD

To complete our survey of Gandhāra sculpture in its Adolescent stage, I append some miscellaneous pieces which admirably illustrate the way in which, from about the middle of the first century onwards, the newly revived Hellenistic art became blended with the Indian. So far as my information goes all the sculptures in this miscellaneous group are made either of grey micaceous schist or of chloritic micaceous schist. The first of them (fig. 78) used to be in the possession of the Church Missionary Society at Peshāwar, but has now, I understand, been donated to the

Peshāwar Museum. It is made of grey micaceous schist and appears to be the lowest block of a jamb belonging to a false niche. The grape-vine scrolls and the bead-and-reel and imbricated leaf-moulding are purely Greek patterns, but there are two features which have clearly been inspired by Buddhist work of the Early Indian School. One is the palmette-like lotus plant at the base of the outer vine-scroll on the left. This is the abbreviated form of the Lotus Tree of Life and Fortune, frequently seen on monuments of the Early Indian School, like the gateways of the Great Stūpa at Sāñchī. The other is the male figure at the base of the larger vine-scroll, who despite his Greek tunic is obviously meant for a *yaksha* of the same class as those portrayed on the gateways at Sāñchī with gift-bearing lotuses either held in their hands or issuing from their mouths or navels.

In fig. 79, which comes from the Dharmarājikā Stūpa at Taxila, Indian influence is more pronounced. This, also, is a fragmentary jamb, and made of chloritized micaceous schist. As in the preceding example, the elaborate mouldings enriching the surface and the Corinthian pilasters and cornices framing the panels are indisputably Greek, but the vertical line of superposed panels is a familiar motif of Early Indian art (cf. figs. 9 above and 149 below) which has persisted down to the present day. And the pairs of figures in each of the panels are also characteristically Indian and attired in Indian costumes (cf. *Taxila*, vol. II, p. 704, no. 23).

The same blending of Greek and Indian features is to be seen in the highly ornate fragment of a frieze reproduced in fig. 80. This, too, comes from the Dharmarājikā Stūpa and, like the foregoing, is made of chloritized micaceous schist. In the upper section is a richly carved vine-scroll of a typically Greek pattern and of great beauty.[1] Below, is an arcade of three pointed arches resting on dwarf Corinthian pilasters. The busts in Indian attire beneath the arches evidently represent gods looking out from the balcony of heaven, as in other Gandhāra reliefs, the figure with long hair under the central arch being Brahmā, and the one on the left Indra, who is wearing the same head-dress as in fig. 84. In the triangular spaces above the haunches of the arches are birds facing front with outspread wings—a common motif in Gandhāra art.

The next piece, fig. 81, is another fragment of a frieze, enriched with

[1] For somewhat similar scroll-work in Apulia, almost certainly inspired by Greek originals, see A. W. Lawrence, *Later Greek Sculpture*, pl. 90*b*.

pure Greek ornament. Although it shows no trace of Indianization I have included it here, because it comes from the same find-spot and is made of the same chloritic micaceous schist as the last two specimens, and because the ornament is of a peculiarly distinctive pattern. On the face of the frieze are two intertwined vine-stems forming a *nodus herculeus*, with four-petalled flowers in the spaces between; and above this, at the dividing line between frieze and cornice, is a band of the tongue-and-dart pattern surmounted by a narrower bead-and-reel moulding.

The above reliefs may be judged to belong to the early part of the Adolescent Period, that is, to about the middle or third quarter of the first century A.D. In the two following pieces (figs. 82, 83), the process of Indianization has gone substantially further. The two are companion pieces from a monument at Kāfir-kot, and are in precisely the same style, and made of the same grey micaceous schist. In fig. 82, a Nāga-rāja is seen seated on his throne beneath his canopy of multiple snake heads, with nāgī musicians and attendants to right and left, each distinguished by the single hood behind her head. The hoods are not very convincing but a comparison with other sculptures of the same kind leaves no doubt as to what they were intended to represent. The other piece (fig. 83) is a drinking scene of the favourite type, with the Nāga-rāja and his queen seated in the centre, holding wine-cups in their hands, while attendant nāgīs on either side are bringing other vessels to supply their needs. Nāgas and nāgīs are, of course, essentially Indian concepts, but both of these scenes are clearly inspired by the drinking and musical scenes of Graeco-Parthian art (e.g. figs. 40, 41, 49, 50, 51 *supra*). Observe that in both reliefs the attendants are wearing Graeco-Parthian wreaths on their heads, and that one of them (next to the Nāga-rāja in fig. 83) is holding up a characteristic Parthian goblet in her fingers in the same peculiar way as one of the male drinkers (third from right) in fig. 40, while another has a drinking horn in her hand. Observe also in fig. 83 the Greek-looking *krater* on the ground, and the man next to it wearing a short Greek *chiton* and carrying a familiar wine-skin over his shoulder. All these features are clearly inspired by Graeco-Parthian prototypes; but on the other hand the dress of both nāgas and nāgīs is Indian rather than Greek, and the anklets worn by the women are typically Indian. Note that the musical instruments are partly Greek, partly Indian.

In the relief which follows (fig. 84) we see once more the essentially

Buddhist character of this art beginning to prevail. The slab portrays the Bodhisattva as a starving and emaciated ascetic before he found true enlightenment. He is seated, yogi-fashion, on a grass-covered throne. The halo behind his head is large and rimmed, like the haloes of the early Buddhas in the Mardān group (e.g. figs. 61, 63, 66), but so far as the mutilation permits one to judge, his *ushṇīsha* appears to be smaller than in those examples. On his left is Brahmā and, behind Brahmā, Indra—recognizable by his distinctive head-dress (cf. fig. 80). Observe his charming, almost girlish, face and the offering of ambrosia which he bears in his hand for the starving Bodhisattva. The lady on the right of the Bodhisattva is no doubt Sujātā, as Foucher rightly divined, with an offering of more human food in her hands. Like Brahmā opposite to her, she is dressed in Greek *chiton* and *himation*, the *chiton* in her case reaching, as usual, to the feet. Behind Sujātā is the Vajrapāṇi in the guise of a Silenus (?), bearded and wreathed with the grape-vine. The workmanship in this relief is a little perfunctory, particularly in respect of the hands and the folds of the drapery. On the other hand, much care and feeling have been expended on the delineation of the faces, and the group as a whole is very attractive—the finest, I think, as it is also the earliest, version of this episode that has come down to us.

I close this chapter on the Adolescent Period with two standing images of the Buddha in the round—the earliest of their kind that the Gandhāra School has bequeathed to us (figs. 85, 86). In the sandstone image, fig. 28, we saw what is probably the earliest of all the known effigies of the Great Teacher, and, in the stucco figures 38 and 39, the earliest known heads of the Bodhisattva. But these were found east of the Indus at Taxila, not west of the river in Gandhāra, and although they throw significant light on the rise of the Gandhāra School, they are not actually products of that School. In Gandhāra itself the oldest representation we possess of the Buddha is the one appearing in fig. 53, where he is distinguished from his companions by nothing more than his halo. That relief, which is essentially Hellenistic in style, dates, as we have seen, from about the middle of the first century A.D. or a little later, i.e. from about the same period as the stucco images of the Bodhisattva referred to above. Approximately contemporary with it, also, are the figures of the infant Bodhisattva to be seen in figs. 55, 57, 58. Then, a decade or so later, comes the Mardān group of reliefs, which show us how the Buddha and

Bodhisattva types were beginning to take shape in the hands of local Buddhist sculptors. It is from the Buddha type as illustrated in those early reliefs that the two statues reproduced in figs. 85 and 86 derive their parentage. The relationship is, indeed, unmistakable. In the statues, as in the reliefs, the Buddha is portrayed wearing a moustache, with eyes wide-open and unduly large *ushṇīsha*. In both, too, his monastic robe is draped in the same way, with its edge falling from wrist or hand in a stiff, straight, or almost straight, line. On the other hand, there are some marked differences. In the reliefs, the halo is of moderate size, while the *ushṇīsha* is so large as to appear top-heavy. In the statues, the halo is disproportionately large, but the *ushṇīsha* is substantially flatter. In the reliefs, again, the drapery folds are roughly modelled and coarsely chiselled; in the statues, the carving is done with great care and precision and with a fine sense for the form beneath the robes. For these differences which are, no doubt, due to improving technique and changing taste, I do not think that more than a couple of decades need be postulated. The Mardān reliefs I ascribe to the beginning of the Adolescent Period, the two statues to a date prior to the Sikri reliefs, which I place at the very end of this period.

These two statues (figs. 85, 86) are so alike that we may well believe that they came from the same atelier, if not from the hand of the same artist. Both the better preserved one (fig. 85) and the other statue (fig. 86), which has lost its halo, part of its *ushṇīsha* and its hands and feet, are in the Lahore Museum.

CHAPTER 8

# PERIOD OF MATURITY

What is meant by 'maturity' in art? The question is one on which views may easily differ. They do so in regard to the art of most countries, ancient and modern; and in the case of Gandhāra art the question is complicated by the fact that the two widely differing types of art, the Indian and the Hellenistic, out of the union of which it was evolved, had long since passed their zenith when it came into being. In consequence of this it happens that some of the earliest reliefs carved for the Buddhists in Gandhāra are, from a plastic and technical point of view, also some of the most perfect. Consider, for example, the group of water deities in fig. 47. There is no later sculpture that can boast of finer workmanship than this; and at one time, indeed, it was regarded as the high-water mark of the Gandhāra School. But the truth is that it is not an example of Gandhāra art at all. Notwithstanding that it was produced on the soil of Gandhāra and carved out of a local stone, it was essentially a work of provincial Greek art, and might properly find a place in any history of that art. This and other reliefs like it are admittedly of great value for the light they shed on the beginnings of Gandhāra art, but only on its beginnings. Gandhāra art is, first and foremost, a Buddhist art, and must be judged by its success in fulfilling its purpose as a sacred art, designed to illustrate the history and legends of the Buddhist faith and to glorify the memory of its Founder. It reached its maturity only when it had evolved a distinctive style and character of its own, and when its sculptors had developed their technical skill and powers of imagination sufficiently to give worthy expression to the traditions and ideals of Buddhism. But the dividing line between adolescence and maturity is, at best, a very hazy one, and arguments might easily be found for shifting it further back or further forward than I have done. Take, for instance, figs. 54 and 55, which come from the same monument and doubtless from the same atelier. Both these reliefs fulfil the requirements of mature art. In both, the workmanship is highly refined and, though they manifestly owe much to Hellenistic teaching, they are already steeped in the spirit of Buddhism and able to tell their stories in a simple, dignified language that well becomes a sacred art. But these reliefs are quite exceptional. They are the work of a school of which we have no other contemporary examples. Had I included them in the present chapter, I should logically have felt constrained to include in it a large number of reliefs of a later date which fall far short of the standard of maturity.

A further complication arises from the fact that the Gandhāra School comprised various groups of ateliers, located in different parts of the country, each with its own traditions and its own individual style. Manifestly these different groups are not likely to have developed on precisely the same lines or at the same rate of progress, and we must be careful, therefore, not to assume that what was true of sculpture in, say, the Chārsada area, was true also of the sculpture of Swāt or Southern Afghānistān. And while making allowance for these local distinctions, we must also take account of the tendency, which is as marked in the case of Gandhāra art as in that of all other sacred art, to perpetuate and even to resuscitate archaic features. Such conservatism may add not a little to the dignity and stability of art, but it has its drawbacks as well as its advantages. Under its influence sculpture is apt to lose its freshness and vitality, to become unimaginative, dull and stereotyped, its beauty giving place to prettiness and its originality to stylishness. This was the fate that overtook Gandhāra sculpture towards the middle of the second century A.D.—only a few decades after reaching maturity—and the effects of it can be seen in the vast mass of uninspired work turned out in Gandhāra during the latter half of that century.

But it would be a mistake to suppose that religious conservatism was the only or, indeed, the chief cause of the nerveless, conventional character of most Gandhāra art dating from this period. Another and perhaps more potent cause was the rapidly growing demand for this sculpture which followed the expansion of Buddhism under Kushān patronage and the ever increasing number of stūpas and chapels which then came into being. In such conditions, when quantity is more important than quality, art of any kind, and particularly religious art, is bound to become repetitive and mechanical. Hence it is that in the later work of this mature period we miss almost entirely the signs of individual genius and of that fresh spontaneous artistry that charmed us in the earlier.

And here we must take note of another significant change which happened about this time and which furnishes an instructive landmark in the history of the School. I refer to the widespread adoption of another variety of stone called phyllite in place of the several schists which had previously been in use. Up to the present I have found no example of phyllite among the sculptures of the early and adolescent periods; none, that is to say, that can be referred to an earlier date than the second century A.D. Phyllite appears to have come into use in the opening years of that century and for a few decades to have been employed side by side with other varieties of schists, but thereafter it almost completely ousted every other kind of stone. And, parenthetically, let me make it clear that I am not a geologist and that in the matter of these stones I rely entirely on the identifications furnished by geological experts, who sometimes differ in the matter of nomenclature. It is for this reason that, except in the case of the sculptures from Taxila, I have refrained from specifying the particular variety of stone used, since I deemed it all-important at this stage to avoid any possibility of confusion in this matter. As far as the Taxila collection is concerned, the identification of the stones was done by an eminent specialist of the old Geological Survey of India, Dr Cotter, and I suggest that his nomenclature might well be adopted in any further work that may be done in this field. Notwithstanding that Taxila lies outside the limits of Gandhāra proper, the sculptures recovered there are more representative of the Gandhāra School as a whole than those from any other known site, and the information they supply as to the different kinds of stone in use at different periods is specially enlightening. Of the 199 sculptures examined by Dr Cotter and described by Mr Hargreaves in the second volume of my *Taxila*, 149 are of phyllite, sixteen of chloritized micaceous schist, eighteen of pale grey micaceous schist, two of talcose chloritic schist, two of hornblende-schist, three of quartz-schist, three of pot-stone (impure talc or steatite), two of slate, three of local Tarakī sandstone, one of red Mathurā sandstone.

For what reason phyllite became so popular can only be surmised. From the sculptor's point of view phyllite has no advantage over the other stones. On the contrary, it is more coarsely grained and more fissile, and thus more liable to fracture under the blows of chisel and mallet. It may be inferred, then, that phyllite owed its popularity simply to the fact that it could be obtained more easily and in greater quantities than any of the other stones mentioned above; for the question of supply must have been of primary importance at a time when so many new monasteries and stūpas were being erected. This is a matter on which some further light may be thrown when we have discovered the whereabouts of the quarries from which these various stones were obtained. Meanwhile, the conjecture may be hazarded that the widespread adoption of phyllite was closely connected with the active support given by the Kushān emperor Kanishka to the Buddhist Church. For assuming that there was a shortage, as there may well have been, of suitable stone for the new building programme, the emperor would naturally have made it his business to ensure an adequate supply by developing the most convenient quarries which were then in operation and by providing for the transport of the stone, thus repeating what his predecessor Aśoka had done four centuries earlier, in the case of the Chunar quarries.

However this may have been, it is significant that the general adoption of phyllite in preference to other stones coincided not only with the decline in the style of this sculpture noticed above, but with other notable changes in its history. One of the most outstanding of these was connected with the development of the Buddha and Bodhisattva images. As far as their attitudes, dress and other canonical features are concerned, the types of these images had been largely standardized before the middle of the second century, but it was left to the latter part of that century to produce the highly refined and delicately wrought images for which Gandhāra art is famous. The beauty of these images is rarely a spiritual one. We look in vain for any expression of the deep, thoughtful compassion which distinguishes, for example, the superb fifth-century head of the Bodhisattva from Kālawān (fig. 152).[1] Their beauty is a purely physical one, resulting in the main from their exquisite finish and the meticulous care lavished on the elaboration of their detail. But we must not underestimate the value of this material beauty. It marks an immense advance on the Buddha and Bodhisattva statues of an earlier period, and to those who were as yet unaware of what the skill of the sculptor would one day achieve in the expression of the spiritual, it must have seemed very near to perfection. So striking, indeed, is it that some of these images were referred by that great authority on Buddhist art, the late Alfred Foucher, to the first century B.C.—two hundred years before their actual date—on the ground that they closely approximated in style to the Greek and must

[1] Cf. *Taxila*, vol. II, frontispiece and pp. 338–9, 470.

have been carved at a time when Greek art was still a vital force in the North-West.

In connexion with these sacred images another noteworthy feature that first made its appearance at this time was the small figural relief, illustrative of some familiar Buddhist scene, which was now used to adorn the base of an image in place of the geometric or floral design that had previously served that purpose. Once introduced, the new figural relief soon came into general vogue, and often constitutes a valuable index to the date of the image to which it belongs.

Other minor developments of a decorative or stylistic kind that distinguish the work of this period will be noticed in the descriptions of the individual sculptures. Meanwhile I have, I think, said enough to make it clear that the sculpture of the Mature period falls naturally into two groups or phases, namely, an earlier phase in which the sculptor's work unmistakably reflects his personal taste and imagination, and a later phase in which the sculptor makes perfection of technique his principal aim, and is content, at the cost of his own creative artistry, to ring the changes on stock themes and stock modes of handling them. According to my calculations, the first of these phases lasted for a few decades only, from the close of the first century until about A.D. 140: the second from that date until the break-up of the Kushān Empire three generations later.

## CHAPTER 9

# EARLY MATURITY PERIOD

(FIGS. 87–112)

In the description which follows of typical sculptures belonging to the first phase of the Maturity period I shall start with the Sanghao-Nathu group, some earlier examples of which have already been noticed. Although provincial in character this group has the advantage of being relatively small and compact, with a style that is easily recognizable, and no doubts about the provenance of the pieces; so that the task of arranging them in chronological sequence is much simplified.

Fig. 87,[1] a slab of greyish-white micaceous schist, came from the Upper Monastery at Nathu, and is now in the Calcutta Museum. Like fig. 72, from the Lower Monastery at the same spot, it depicts the death of the Buddha, but is of later date. A comparison of the two panels is instructive. In both the faulty modelling of the eyes is conspicuous, and in both the drapery folds are coarse and rough. These defects are characteristic of the majority of the sculptures belonging to this group and persisted throughout most of its history. On the other hand, there are marked differences between these two panels. In the late one, the limbs of the Buddha have lost all trace of suppleness; he is now like a stiffly frontal statue laid on its side. Moreover, he is provided with a rimmed halo behind his head, and his hands and feet are enveloped in the folds of his robe. As to the group of mourners round the couch, their number has been reduced from twelve to nine by omitting three of the monks, including the prostrate Ānanda; and the Vajrapāṇi, transformed from a robed and bearded man into a half-naked youth (a type we have already encountered among the Sikri sculptures), now takes his place at the head of the couch. But the most significant change is in the faces of the mourners. In fig. 68, the earliest version of the Parinirvāṇa known to us

[1] This is the earliest photograph I possess of this interesting piece. It was taken, I think, some seventy-five years ago when the sculpture was unearthed. In a later photograph, reproduced in Foucher's *A.G.-B.G.* vol. II, fig. 437, the two centre figures on the further side of the couch have lost their heads; and in a still later photograph recently supplied by the Calcutta Museum, the figure on the right of the same row has also lost his head, and the right *śāla* tree has been damaged.

in Gandhāra, the artist was at great pains to show the signs of grief and weeping on their faces. And in fig. 72 the sorrow is still apparent, though there are no actual tears to be seen. But in fig. 87 all trace of sorrow has gone. Every one of the actors—*devas*, monk, chiefs, the Vajrapāṇi, even the dying Buddha himself—wear the same pleasant and fatuous smile. For all that their expressions mean, they might just as well be assisting at a marriage as at a death. We must not, however, deny all merit to the author of this relief. Granted that it possesses no spiritual or emotional significance, yet there is undoubted charm of a decorative kind in the grouping of the figures and in their winsome countenances. I know of no other sculpture in which this particular cast of countenance occurs, and the credit for it, such as it is, must therefore go to the sculptor's personal inventiveness. The pity is that his example pointed the way to that facile duplication of pleasing faces which was to become one of the hall-marks of later Gandhāra art. Yet another noticeable feature of this relief is the exaggerated size of the figures in the back row compared with those in front. This artificial defiance of the laws of perspective can be seen also in fig. 90.

The next relief (fig. 88) also comes from Nathu, and is now in the Calcutta Museum. It illustrates the presentation to the Buddha of a mango grove by the courtesan Āmrapālī. To indicate the occasion, the Buddha is portrayed seated under a canopy of mango leaves and fruit. On his right is Āmrapālī with her lady companions; on his left, two of the Licchavi nobles, and beyond them the Vajrapāṇi and a *deva*. That Āmrapālī is in the act of making a gift is shown by the ceremonial water-vessel in her hands. The wreaths which she and her companions wear on their heads are survivals of the wreaths so fashionable among the upper classes of Graeco-Parthian society. All the figures in this panel, except the Buddha, have the same bulging eyes that we noticed in the preceding relief as well as in figs. 69–72. Evidently the sculptor made a special, though not very successful, effort to avoid this distortion in the case of the Buddha, but when he came to the subsidiary figures, old habit proved too strong for him, as it did also when he was carving the small standing Buddha on the face of the adjacent pilaster. Other noteworthy features of this panel are the heavy canopy of mango leaves, akin to the canopies in figs. 100 and 101 below, as well as to those on some of the Sikri slabs, e.g. fig. 77, and the modelling of the drapery folds, which shows a growing sense of line and substance, though the execution is still uncompromisingly hard. Observe, too, how the ubiquitous *śāla* trees are still introduced, as a cliché to mark the Buddha's presence, though they have nothing to do with the episode of Āmrapālī's gift.

Most of the sculptures from the Sanghao-Nathu area are in the style illustrated by the two foregoing reliefs, but there are not a few from the same area which display a noticeably different style. Two of these are reproduced in figs. 89 and 90. The former, which is of greyish-white micaceous schist, comes from the Upper Monastery at Nathu and is now in the Calcutta Museum. It represents a *yakshī* standing beneath a *śāla* tree. Such *yakshī* figures were common enough in Gandhāra art, but it was only in the Sanghao-Nathu area that they acquired the ultra-smart and fashionable appearance of this figure. The pose under the *śāla* tree is much the same as that of Māyā in the Birth scene. The wreath on her head was, as already noticed, of Graeco-Parthian origin, but in other respects her dress and ornaments are Indian. The former consist of a *dhotī*, long-sleeved jacket or coatee and scarf; the latter of a forehead medallion, ear-rings, two necklaces, crossed breast-chain (of which only the top is visible), hip-girdle, wrist bangles and anklets. But the most striking feature of this *yakshī* is her long, slanting eyes, all the more striking because they are so completely different from the bulging eyes which normally distinguished the sculptures of this group. What, one wonders, was the artist's reason for introducing this strange new feature? Was it simply because of the difficulty he and his fellow artists had to model the natural Indian eye? Or was it because he aimed at giving his *yakshī* a look that was not quite human, as her nature might seem to demand? Probably the latter is the true answer; for it is not long after this that a somewhat similar though less accentuated treatment is found in images of the Buddha, and in their case it can hardly be doubted that the sculptors fully appreciated the value of these weird un-Indian eyes in giving the Buddha a far-away, unearthly and superhuman look without unduly conflicting with his otherwise formal features. Nor can we doubt that it was this suggestion of other-worldliness in the half-closed eyes that caused its almost universal adoption for the Buddha's images throughout the Buddhist world, though the expansion of Buddhism to the Middle and Far East, where Mongolian eyes are the rule rather than the exception, has doubtless been an important factor in perpetuating this characteristic feature until the present day.

One other detail of this interesting *yakshī* statue that calls for a passing remark is the light scarf wound in flowing curves round her right shoulder and arm. Scarves treated in this flowing fashion were used effectively as ornamental adjuncts in many sculptures belonging to this group (e.g. *A.M.I.* pls. 113–15) as well as in earlier sculptures of the Graeco-Parthian group (e.g. fig. 44 above).

The second example of this particular style (fig. 90) is a fragment of chloritized micaceous schist, which was found at Loriyān Tangai and is now in the Calcutta Museum. I have included it here because it furnishes another illustration of the ornamental scarf alluded to above, and also shows the effect which the slanting eyes were beginning to have on the more normal modelling of that feature. Of what scene this small fragment formed a part is questionable, but perhaps a clue may be given by the *deva* at the back with two fingers to his lips as if in the act of whistling. A similar figure, making the same gesture of rejoicing, occurs in the Birth scene illustrated in *A.G.-B.G.* vol. I, fig. 154, p. 306. For the exaggerated size of the figures in the back row compare figs. 87 above and 95 below.[1]

There remains the ornamental base reproduced in fig. 91. This fragment, which is now in the Calcutta Museum, is known to have come from the Lower Monastery at Nathu, but, even if we had not known this, we should have had a safe clue to its provenance in the large bulging eyes of the *devas* and Erotes. The motif of the 'garland and Erotes' was of Hellenistic origin and was widely diffused throughout Western Asia, including Gandhāra, where it became a prime favourite in the second and third centuries A.D. The basis of the design is a row of Erotes (*yakshas*) supporting an undulating garland on their shoulders, but there is much variety in the accessories and details. In its simplest and earliest form, the garland is of the imbricated-leaf pattern, but later on this pattern is elaborated by binding the garland at intervals with ribbons and enriching it with various foliate and other designs (cf. fig. 148 and *Taxila*, vol. II, p. 709, nos. 72, 73, and vol. III, pl. 216). Again, the Erotes are generally nude with necklaces and Indian anklets only to relieve their nudity, but in rare cases they wear a loin cloth, in others they have no anklets. At the bottom of the loops between the Erotes there usually hang bunches of fruit, or fruit and leaves, but occasionally these are omitted; and the

[1] Cf. also *Monuments of Sāñchī*, vol. II, pl. XXXVI *c*.

spaces immediately above them are, in most examples, occupied by winged *devas* or *devīs*, but in other examples by birds with outstretched wings or bunches of leaves. Such features are helpful in determining the age of individual pieces. In fig. 91, the Erotes or *yakshas* are standing to the front, wearing Indian anklets and holding cymbals and drum in their hands. The garland is of the simple imbricated-leaf pattern, with bunches of fruit at the bottom of its folds, while in the spaces above are winged figures playing on stringed instruments. Taken together, these features denote a fairly early date for this composition, and it is certainly earlier than fig. 148, but I do not think that it can be placed much before the close of the early phase of the Maturity Period. More will be said on this subject when we come to deal with fig. 148.

From the foregoing sculptures of the provincial Sanghao-Nathu group we turn to those which are more in the main current of Gandhāra art. These comprise several distinct styles, which anyone familiar with the subject will easily recognize, but there is little or no evidence to show to which particular localities they appertained. That one important centre was located at Pushkalāvatī (modern Chārsada), the ancient capital of Gandhāra, is, on the face of it, highly probable and is borne out by the exceptionally good quality of some of the reliefs found on that spot. It has long been recognized, too, that other important centres of activity were situated in the Swāt Valley and in the neighbourhood of Haḍḍa in Southern Afghānistān; and it may safely be assumed that, after the transfer of the capital from Pushkalāvatī to Purushapura (modern Peshāwar), yet another centre was developed at the latter city. But we are still very much in the dark about these different local groups, and about others also that must have existed in the remoter parts of the Peshāwar Valley and adjacent hill tracts, wherever stone suitable for this kind of sculpture was procurable and enough Buddhist settlements existed to maintain a steady demand for the sculpture. For the present, therefore, and until more information on the subject is available, we must be content to differentiate where we can between the several styles, and leave it to others to determine where each of them was evolved.

Of the sculptures of this period which I have selected for illustration, one of the earliest is fig. 92—a small relief of chloritic schist, now in the British Museum, which is alleged to have come from Takht-i-Bahī. The scene portrayed is the 'Sleep of the women'. In the centre is the princess

Yaśodharā asleep on a cushioned couch, her hand under her cheek and a garland still on her head. Beside her, sitting on the side of the couch, is her husband the Bodhisattva, haloed and in princely attire. At the side of the couch, in the foreground, the ladies of the palace have fallen asleep over their drums. At the back, on the right, are a female guard and attendant; on the left, presumably the groom Chandaka carrying his master's head-dress and leading the horse Kaṇṭhaka by the bridle, but these two figures are too damaged to be identified with certainty. Framing the scene on either side are two Corinthian pilasters with rounded shafts in countersunk panels, like those in figs. 43–7, 54, 55, etc., but of later form. In design and workmanship the panel leaves much to be desired, but it is not without considerable charm, and in spite of its shortcomings—the stilted pose, for example, of the Bodhisattva with his feet dangling over the side of the bed, and the careless, unsteady chiselling of the drapery folds—it is evident that the artist has made a genuine effort to bring his imagination into play and to express in his own way the overpowering effect of the heaven-sent slumber which took possession of the womenfolk on the night the Bodhisattva fled from the palace. Stylistically the relief has much in common with fig. 58, and more remotely with figs. 54 and 55, but its date is later and the influence of the Early Indian School is more apparent in the decorative, tapestry-like grouping of the figures. The sleepers' smooth and pretty faces, too, like those already noticed in fig. 87, are a foretaste of what, a generation later, was to become one of the most familiar features of Gandhāra art. But for these traits, the relief might well have been referred to the preceding period. As it is, I think we must give it a place at the outset of the Maturity period. Another and later relief in the British Museum illustrating the same theme is reproduced in *A.G.-B.G.* vol. II, fig. 447, but the design is much inferior and the postures of the sleeping women could hardly be more uncomely.

In my excavations at the Dharmarājikā Stūpa at Taxila I found several fragments of much larger panels depicting the same 'Sleeping Women' scene[1] (cf. *Taxila*, vol. II, pp. 713–14, nos. 98–100), one of which is shown in fig. 93. It exhibits three sleeping figures, with traces of a fourth at the right-hand top corner. One of the three is seated on a high-backed

[1] The stone of these panels has been identified with phyllite by one expert, as chloritized micaceous schist by another.

wicker chair with legs crossed and arm bent to support her drooping head; another, on the left, rests her head against her hand; the third, in the background, holds a six-stringed instrument. In this, as in other fragments of the same kind from the Dharmarājikā, the shapes of the women are strikingly rounded and full, and their thin clinging draperies serve well to reveal the lines of their figures. This marks a new development in Gandhāra art. Roughly speaking, there are two diametrically opposite methods of representing the folds of drapery. One, which was the normal Greek method, was to cut away the mass of the fabric, leaving the folds projecting from the surface, as they naturally do. The other method, which was commonly favoured by Roman sculptors, was to indicate the folds merely by deep-cut shadow lines, leaving the mass of material between them intact. Of these two methods it was the Greek one that was universally followed by the sculptors of Gandhāra in the first and second centuries A.D. and, whatever variations were introduced, the underlying principle remained the same. Thus, if we compare fig. 93 with, for example, fig. 57, we see that in both cases the sculptor was following the Greek practice, the only difference between them being that, whereas in the earlier work the draperies were thicker and looser and the folds more numerous and heavy, in the later the draperies were thin and tight-fitting while the folds were kept sparse and slight so as to bring out the shapeliness of the forms beneath and interfere as little as possible with the clarity of the composition as a whole. And an added advantage, of course, was that this treatment reduced the labour of chiselling to a minimum without unduly sacrificing either charm or effectiveness. In the above generalization I have naturally not taken account of the hasty and slovenly method of depicting draperies exemplified in figs. 58 and 59, where superficially incised lines are used, with a sort of pictorial effect, to represent the folds.

The light and sketchy treatment of the women's dress which distinguishes fig. 93 is to be seen in a panel of phyllite depicting Māyā's dream, which was found in the Kālawān monastery at Taxila (fig. 94). Occupying the centre of the picture is the queen's bedchamber, flanked by vaulted corridors supported on Persepolitan pillars. In the middle of the chamber Māyā is lying asleep on a draped couch, her head raised on a high pillow. Beside her, at the head of the couch, stands a female attendant, while another, spear in hand, keeps guard at the foot and two more wait in the vaulted corridors. To the right, above the queen's head, is a gallery, from which two seated figures, presumably *devas*, are looking down, and to the left of it the defaced stone shows the outline of the haloed Bodhisattva descending in the form of an elephant. The legs of the queen's couch are carved to represent the stylized fronts of horned animals. The pillars supporting the roof are of the Persepolitan order but, strange to say, they were never provided with shafts. This is evident from the fact that the base of the pillar on the right is not vertically in line with the bell capital above. The style of the relief is unusual. In the architectural setting and disposition of the figures the sculptor has followed an established tradition; and in the modelling of the well-developed forms and comely faces of the women and even in depicting one of the attendants with her back to the spectator he has done only what other artists at this period were doing; but in other essential factors of the design—in the unusually open spacing of the figures and the simplified refinement of the details, which combine to give a quiet dignity and charm to this relief—he has drawn on his own originality and good taste. For further particulars, cf. *Taxila*, vol. II, p. 712, no. 92, and vol. III, pl. 218, no. 92.

We now come to some miscellaneous pieces which are referable to this period but cannot easily be linked with any particular group. Among them I give an early and prominent place to fig. 95, which was formerly in the possession of Maj.-Gen. H. L. Haughton, but is now, I believe, in the Victoria and Albert Museum in London. Mr Hargreaves, who published it in the *Journal of the Royal Asiatic Society* (1951, pp. 131–3 and pl. IV), is clearly right in interpreting it as the child Bodhisattva going to school in a ram-cart, accompanied by his school-fellows carrying their writing-boards and ink-pots. At first sight, the relief might appear to belong rather to the close of the Adolescent Period than to the beginning of this one, but the sketchy treatment of the boys' tunics, coupled with the highly refined modelling of their young faces and of the rams' heads, and the slight stylization of the indispensable *śāla* tree in the corner—all point to the later date. A prominent feature of this panel is the exaggerated size of the four figures in the background in relation to those in front. This disregard of the laws of perspective has already been noticed in connexion with figs. 87 and 90, but it is rare in Gandhāra reliefs, and does not appear to be a trait of any particular group. In this case, the author's main concern has been with the minutiae of the individual figures rather than with the composition as a whole, and it was probably for this reason that he went out of his way to show the four figures in the background on an exaggerated scale. Had they been in correct perspective, they would have been too small for him to display his skill in varying the details of their features and hair-dressing. The relief is said to have been found in the Chārsada Tehsil of the Peshāwar District.

A hint as to the district which may have produced the preceding sculptures is afforded by some fragmentary reliefs found by Professor Vogel and myself at Chārsada in 1902–3 and particularly by the phyllite panel illustrated in fig. 96, which was found in the ruins of Palātu-Dheṛī. What is left of it comprises seven partly mutilated figures, namely, the Buddha standing in the centre, with the Vajrapāṇi and a monk on his right, two *devas* above them in the background, and two other headless figures on the Buddha's left. The episode in the Buddha's career which is here portrayed has not been identified and there is no need for us to speculate about it here. What concerns us is the masterly handling of the drapery, which though fuller and more elaborately modelled than in the two preceding examples, is designed like them to show off the natural shapes underneath. Which of them is the earlier it would be difficult to say, but it is noteworthy that the *deva* head behind the Buddha's right shoulder is of the same moustached type as those we encountered in figs. 59, 62, 68, and though manifestly posterior to them, points to a relatively early date for this relief.

The same type of moustached *deva* head may be seen in fig. 97—a small panel of chloritic schist which is now in the British Museum. In this case the *deva* heads are more closely akin to those of the Adolescent Period, and this affinity is borne out by the treatment of the drapery. On the other hand, the short stocky figures and individualistic faces of the worshippers point to a near relationship with sculptures of this period such as fig. 98. The subject depicted in this relief is the 'Adoration of a stūpa', and we should note, in passing, the continuous garland supported on brackets which adorns the base of the dome—a motif to which reference has already been made. On the right of the stūpa are a male and a female lay-worshipper, the former holding an incense-burner; on the left, two shaven monks. Above, in the background, are six *devas*, the two nearest the stūpa with haloes and lotuses in their hands. Four of the six have their faces mutilated.

The label attached to this panel in the British Museum states that it was given to the museum in 1902 by Captain B. C. Waterfield and that it came from Buner. This must, I think, be a mistake, since the sculpture is one of a group which was photographed in the Swāt Valley some years before 1902.[1]

The following relief (fig. 98) comes from the Dharmarājikā Stūpa at Taxila and is of phyllite stone. The scene depicted has not been identified. In the centre sits the Buddha enthroned, in the *abhaya-mudrā*, with the Vajrapāṇi and seven female devotees on his right and left. The Buddha wears a moustache, the Vajrapāṇi a bushy beard as well as a moustache. Of the devotees, three—a young mother and two children—stand on the Buddha's right; the other four on his left—two elderly ones in front and two middle-aged behind. The figures are of much the same stocky build as those in the preceding relief and are distinguished by the same highly realistic countenances. But there is a noticeable difference in the treatment of the eyes; for, whereas in fig. 97 the eyes are more or less normal in shape, here they are pear-shaped and slanting, not unlike those of the *yakshī* in fig. 89. As in the case of fig. 89, this unwonted shape of the eye was doubtless intended to give the countenance an other-worldly, superhuman look, and it is reasonable to assume that in adopting it the artist was thinking primarily of the Buddha, and that he subsequently extended it to some other members of the group.

In fig. 3, above, we saw how a sculptor of the Early School portrayed the Birth of the Buddha by setting the figure of his mother, Māyā, on a lotus (the symbol of miraculous birth), with two Nāga elephants pouring the lustral water over her head. The picture was a formal and symbolic one, but as good, perhaps, as could be devised in an age when it was not permissible to represent the person of the Buddha himself. Here, in fig. 99, we see the more graphic and realistic way in which a sculptor of the Gandhāra School was able to portray the same event. In the centre, Māyā is standing under a *śāla* tree and grasping one of its branches. On her right are four deities, one of whom is delivering the infant from the side of his mother, while the rest look on in reverential attitudes. Balancing the deities on the other side of Māyā are her lady companions: first, her sister Mahāprajāpatī, who is supporting her; then

[1] Cf. *Catalogue of Photo-negatives in the Office of the Director-General of Archaeology in India* (Calcutta, 1920), p. 218, no. 2355.

a lady carrying a vessel of lustral water, and, behind her, a maid, gazing in astonishment at what is happening. Above the group are celestials, adoring the new-born Buddha. This nativity scene is the subject of many Gandhāra sculptures, some more abbreviated than this one, but all conforming more or less to the same stereotype pattern. Among them I know of only one that is of earlier date than fig. 99, namely, a panel from the Guides' Mess at Mardān, which is in precisely the same style as figs. 54 and 55 above and, like them, referable to the Adolescent Period. In all these other reliefs, both early and late, the deity playing the part of midwife is recognizable as Indra, and the one next to him as Brahmā. This was strictly in accord with the version of the Nativity story current in Gandhāra. But there was another version, found in the Pāli scriptures, in which the Regents of the Four Quarters took the place of Indra and Brahmā, and it is evidently this version which, by exception, was followed in fig. 99, where the deities on the right of Māyā are four in number and are all wearing the same head-dress.

Another noteworthy feature of this carving is the pretty but doll-like and rather fatuous expression on the ladies' faces. It is a feature to which I have already drawn attention in several earlier reliefs, notably, figs. 87, 88, 92 and 93, and a feature to which we shall frequently have to recur, as it assumes increasingly greater importance in the later phases of the School.

We may now turn to another group of contemporary sculptures in a markedly different style, several examples of which were found at the Dharmarājikā Stūpa at Taxila. A characteristic feature of this group is the tall athletic build of the male figures, with powerful sloping shoulders, strong hips and thighs, tapering legs and rather small ankles and feet. Another characteristic is the somewhat sketchy nature of the drapery, frequently distinguished by the shallow flattened edges of its folds. A third characteristic, but one which is not confined to these sculptures alone, is the highly elaborated canopy of leaves over the throne of the Buddha. The three examples of this group figured below are all of phyllite stone and all from the Dharmarājikā Stūpa. The scene depicted in the first of them (fig. 100) appears to be the miracle at the foot of the mango tree at Śrāvastī, also depicted in figs. 122–5. Under a canopy of mango leaves the Buddha is seated on a grass-strewn throne, his right hand turned outwards above his knee. On his left, King Prasenajit is sitting on a cushioned seat with his courtiers behind. On his right is the faithful Vajrapāṇi in monkish garb, and in front of the Vajrapāṇi two naked *tīrthaṅkaras*, one seated on a round stool, the other—a man of singularly ill-favoured looks—standing. For the earlier version of the miracle which seems to be followed here, see *Monuments of Sāñchī*, pl. xxxiv, A, 1.

The next example (fig. 101) may well be from the same atelier as the preceding though not, I judge, by the same hand. The scene represented is uncertain. In the centre is the Buddha under a canopy of pipal leaves. On his right is a bearded anchorite clad in a deerskin and holding a flask (*kamaṇḍalu*) in his hand, who calls to mind the familiar figure of the Purāṇa Kāśyapa. On the Buddha's left is a princely-looking personage, standing erect with his right hand outstretched as if in salutation, while his courtier behind clasps his hands in adoration. In the background behind is the headless figure of a *deva*. The relief is much damaged and the face of the Buddha is obliterated, but the tall dignified figure of the prince with its elegant proportions, strong frame and tapering legs, furnishes a typical example of this particular group.

The third example (fig. 102) presents an unusual scene. In the centre, the Bodhisattva, who has the attributes of Maitreya, the future Buddha, is seated cross-legged on his throne under an elaborate baldachin. His right hand is raised in the *abhaya-mudrā*, his left holds a flask. The roof of the baldachin is supported on tall pillars, to the upper halves of which winged Erotes or *yakshas* are clinging. To the right and left of the throne is a haloed deity seated, European fashion, on a chair, and standing behind them are other figures, now much mutilated but one at least of whom can be recognized by his halo as a celestial. The scene has been interpreted as the *saṃcodana* or Entreaty, when the gods besought the Bodhisattva to leave his princely home and family in Kapilavastu in order to become the Buddha and save mankind, but it seems more likely to represent that other occasion in the Tushita heaven when the gods entreated the future Buddha to return to earth. I make this suggestion because, if the scene was laid at Kapilavastu, we should have expected the Bodhisattva to be shown in his usual princely attire. On the other hand, if it was in the Tushita heaven, it was natural that he should be represented as Maitreya. The two seated deities may be Indra and Brahmā, but they are too mutilated to allow of certain identification. It is in these two seated deities in particular, with their well-proportioned build, tapering legs and small feet, that we recognize the close connexion with the two preceding reliefs.

Of about the same age as the foregoing and closely akin to them in the athletic build of the figures is a group of sculptures from Jamāl-Garhī, one of the earlier Buddhist foundations in Gandhāra. Three examples of these will suffice to demonstrate the emphasis laid on physical development. Fig. 103 is a part of a stele or *urdhvapatta* of greyish-white micaceous schist. The scene in the upper panel has not been identified; that in the lower is a later edition of fig. 69, namely, the submission of the Nāga Apalāla. But the artistry of the reliefs is of a very different order. In the earlier (fig. 69) the artist has given us a lively and dramatic picture of the incident, with little regard for the forms of the individual figures. In the later, he has paid as much attention to the correct anatomical modelling of each figure as to the effectiveness of the composition as a whole, and has imparted to his work a certain heroic quality which is seldom found outside this group. The same high standard is maintained in fig. 104, which tells so simply and convincingly the story of the simultaneous birth of the Bodhisattva's groom Chandaka and of his horse Kaṇṭhaka. The scene is set in the royal stables. There, side by side, we see the mother of Chandaka bathing her new-born child, and the dam of Kaṇṭhaka giving milk to her foal, while she herself receives a bran-mash from the hand of a royal groom; and in the background are the heads of other horses watching the double event from their stalls. The seated figure of the mother, with her well-developed limbs and refined, delicately chiselled face, is in keeping with other sculptures of this group, but there is no close parallel that I know of to the animals. The sympathetic feeling that the artist has put into their modelling calls to mind the two horses' heads on the East Gateway of the Great Stūpa at Sāñchī (fig. 8 above), though the style of the latter is very different.

It is a pity that the next panel (fig. 105), depicting the wrestling match, is marred by the exaggerated forms of the two combatants in the foreground, due to the superhuman stature of the Bodhisattva, on which the sculptor no doubt thought it necessary to insist. Apart from this blemish the relief affords another good example of the importance which, in this group of sculptures, was attached to the athletic development of the human form, coupled with a highly refined miniature-like treatment of the facial features. A comparison of the muscular figure on the left side of the panel with the *yaksha* hurling the thunderbolt in the top left corner of fig. 103 suggests that the two reliefs may have emanated from the same atelier.

Jamāl-Garhī, where the foregoing sculptures were found, has yielded many more of the same age which would well repay closer study. Parenthetically, it may be noted that Jamāl-Garhī was originally laid out on the same circular plan as the Dharmarājikā at Taxila, as distinguished from the later rectangular plans of such foundations as Jauliāñ, Mohṛā Morādu or Takht-i-Bahī. Hence the large number of relatively early as well as late sculptures which Jamāl-Garhī, like the Dharmarājikā, has yielded, though it should be added that the Dharmarājikā was founded long before Jamāl-Garhī.

Among the many miscellaneous reliefs of this period, which it is difficult to link up with any particular group, two of the most noteworthy are figs. 106 and 107. The former, a narrow frieze of phyllite from the Dharmarājikā at Taxila, has been sadly damaged, but enough remains to give a fair idea of its character. The story it recounts is the same Śyāma Jātaka that we met with in fig. 10*a*. Here, the method of narration is in the Greek, not in the Indian, tradition. That is to say, the actors in the successive scenes are strung out in single file, as they habitually were in the friezes of Greek temples, though not strictly in chronological sequence. The right end of the frieze is missing, and the first act that we see is the king in hunting dress drawing his bow and an attendant behind him holding a quiver full of arrows. The wildness of the country is shown by the usual conventional rocks and vegetation, with a lion's head peering out from a cave. Then, beyond the rocks to the left, we see the boy Śyāma sinking to the ground with an arrow in his breast. In the next act, which shows the god Indra restoring the boy to life, Indra appears haloed and floating in the air with a flask of ambrosia in his hand, while the reviving Śyāma raises his hands above his head and the king looks on impassively. On the left of the frieze the figure of the king is twice more repeated; first, visiting the boy's blind and aged parents in their leafy hut and informing them, with appropriate gesture of the fingers, of what has happened to their son, and then leading them painfully to the scene of the miracle. The figures of the blind old couple are quite realistic and convincing, but the sculptor has clearly, in this case, been more concerned about the telling of the story, act by act, than about the modelling of the form or the delicate refinement of details. Indian influence, be it added, is somewhat more marked in the individual figures of this frieze than in most of the contemporary sculpture.

The other relief (fig. 107), which comes from the monastery of Giri at Taxila, is without parallel in the Gandhāra School. It depicts the visit of Indra to the Buddha in the Indraśaila cave. The panel is divided horizontally by a railing into two compartments. In the lower, the Buddha is seated in meditation inside the cave, his hands and feet hidden in the folds of his robe. Outside the cave, on the Buddha's left, stands Indra, recognizable by his tall hat; and opposite to him, on the Buddha's right, Brahmā. Both deities are haloed. As if to accentuate the wildness of the spot, two pigs appear among the rocks in front of the cave. In the upper compartment four *devas*, like wingless angels, are emptying baskets of flowers over the front of the cave, two swooping down headlong with lithe and graceful forms, the other two bending gently forward and filling the space between them. And note, in passing, how skilfully the flying ends of the *devas*' scarves are used to enhance the sense of rapid movement as well as to indicate, as they do in figs. 89, 90 and 106, that the figures are of celestial birth. The pretty but rather meaningless faces of the four *devas* are akin to those already noticed in figs. 87, 88, 92, 94, 95 and 99, but the rhythmic grouping of the celestial figures and the happy conception of their flowery tribute to the Buddha are unique in Gandhāra art. Indeed, the nearest counterpart to the wingless angels is to be found, according to M. Foucher, in the Portail Royal of Chartres Cathedral (A.D. 1145–50).

There remain only a few examples of detached images to be considered. The first of these (fig. 108) is a *yaksha* Atlant of the Herakles type, one of a number of such Atlants said to have come from Jamāl-Garhī and now in the Calcutta Museum. It is made of the grey micaceous schist much in use at this period, and in spite of its diminutive size (it is less than 8 in. high), is a skilful and vigorous bit of modelling. Like figs. 52 and 145, it takes its lineage from Greek prototypes, but the differences between the three are very striking. The earliest (fig. 52), a Silenus-like winged figure, is the embodiment of strength in repose, in this respect contrasting with the Indian *yakshas* of fig. 12, which display not only giant strength but dynamic energy as well in their effort to uphold the superincumbent mass. In fig. 52, the *yaksha* is making no effort at all to bring his great muscles into play; he is merely squatting pleasantly at his ease. The same is true of the Herakles-like *yaksha* of fig. 108, but in this instance the artist has been at pains to give clearer definition to the facial features and muscular development of the limbs, and in other respects to keep as near as possible to his Hellenistic prototype; and his little figurine certainly does him credit. That such a purely classical type should have persisted on into the Maturity Period may, at first sight, seem surprising, but to the end Gandhāra art remained very partial to the use of Greek types and motifs. Thus, among the many members of the Greek pantheon represented among the sculptures of this period may be mentioned Zeus, Athene, Hermes, Dionysus and Eros, to say nothing of the countless little Erotes or Amorini used for decorative purposes. But when we come to the later part of the Maturity Period, we shall see, in fig. 145, a striking example of how such types could be affected by the growing tendency towards prettiness and effeminacy.

In chapter 7 we have seen that the earliest known statues of the Buddha in the round, or virtually in the round, were the two illustrated in figs. 85 and 86, which like contemporary figures of the Buddha in relief were distinguished by wide-open prominent eyes, moustache, *ūrṇā*, large *ushṇīsha* and halo, and a monastic robe (*saṅghāṭī*) resembling the Greek *himation*. With figs. 109, 110 and 111 we again take up the story of the Buddha statue. The head and torso shown in fig. 110, which is now in the Lahore Museum, is 3 ft. 5 in. high and of grey micaceous schist, possibly chloritized. Its affinity to figs. 85 and 86 is manifest. It has the same kind of moustache, with *ūrṇā* and large flat *ushṇīsha*, the same treatment of the hair even to the thin cord confining it round the base of the *ushṇīsha*, the same outsize halo and the same draping of the *saṅghāṭī*. The main difference is in the eyes, which are now half-closed, giving them that far-away, other-worldly look which was eventually to become one of the standard traits of the Buddha type. But at the time this image was carved, there was still much vacillation among the Gandhāran sculptors about this particular feature. And so it happens that in this statue the eyelids are drawn close together, while in the two following examples they are left open. Indeed, it is true, I think, to say that throughout the first phase of the Maturity Period the treatment of the eyelids was a matter for the personal discretion of the artist, not one of canonical rule.

To judge by the shape of the *ushṇīsha* and the less schematic treatment of the hair, fig. 109 is somewhat later than the foregoing, but the evidence is not conclusive. The eyes are wide-open but not prominent, as in figs. 85 and 86, and the pupils are defined; the *ūrṇā* is higher up the forehead than in the preceding figure; round the base of the *ushṇīsha* is a double string of beads with a medallion in front. The head, which has lost its ears and halo, is made of talcose chloritic schist. It came from the Mohṛā Morādu Monastery at Taxila.

Between the next statue (fig. 111) and fig. 110 there is little apparent difference except in the eyes and in the quality of the workmanship, which is hardly up to the same standard. It is also significant that the material is not the usual micaceous schist of which most of the early sculptures of this period are made, but phyllite, which was just coming into use. The statue came from the Dharmarājikā Stūpa at Taxila.

I conclude this chapter with a figure of Hāritī, consort of Pāñcika, which seems to sum up well the character of the Early Maturity Period (fig. 112). The panel, which is now in the Peshāwar Museum, came originally from Takht-i-Bahī, where it no doubt served as a spacer between larger panels in the decoration of a stūpa. Such spacers, adorned with figures of female guards, musicians, etc., like those in figs. 64, 65, were a common feature of Gandhāra art from an early date. In this example (fig. 112) the *devī* is shown standing erect on a vase under a canopy of leaves. Her dress is Indian; her ornaments are necklaces, bracelets and anklets. On her head is a chaplet of leaves, from which a veil falls down her back. On her left hip she carries, in the local fashion, the youngest of her many children. The figure of Hāritī is, as usual, full and matronly; her pose dignified and stately, giving her a madonna-like appearance. Of the age of this carving, its restrained classic style and the maturity of the modelling leave no room for doubt; for it was only in the early part of the Maturity Period that work of this calibre was produced. For the ungainly treatment of the lower folds of Hāritī's veil, which resemble the shape of acanthus leaves, compare the decoration of a small stūpa in Sirkap (*Taxila*, vol. III, pl. 27 (*a*)) and on an early statuette of grey mica-schist from the Dharmarājikā (*ibid.* pl. 226, no. 179). See also the contemporary relief, fig. 101 above. For further details of the cult of Hāritī, cf. Foucher, *A.G.-B.G.* vol. II, pp. 130–42 and figs. 374–8.

## CHAPTER 10

# LATER MATURITY PERIOD: RELIEFS

(FIGS. 113–30)

We have now reached the most fertile and best-known period in the history of Gandhāra art—the period covered by the three generations between A.D. 140 or thereabouts, and the break-up of the Kushān Empire. It was the period that produced the bulk of the sculptures usually found in public and private collections, and we shall see how the vastly increased output was accompanied by a creeping deterioration of style; how originality and inventiveness rapidly gave place to conventionalism, and artistry to craftsmanship. But we shall see, also, that the new craftsmanship retained a perfection undreamt of by earlier sculptors; we shall note many attractive, albeit oft-recurring, motifs and patterns; and we shall be charmed by the pervading prettiness of the faces, divine and human.

In the series of illustrations which follows, I have given the first two places to figs. 113 and 114, because they appear to mark the transition from the earlier to the later phase of the Maturity Period. The former (fig. 113) is representative of a small but highly interesting group of reliefs, of which, had it been possible, I would gladly have included more examples. Fortunately, four other pieces belonging to this group have already been published elsewhere. One of them, a fragment depicting the 'Birth Scene' from Loriyān Tangai, can be seen in Foucher's *L'art gréco-bouddhique*, vol. I, fig. 154; the remaining three in *Ancient Monuments of India*, figs. 97, 100, 136; fig. 100 was found in the Nathu monastery; the provenance of the others is unknown; but their style is so similar that there can be little doubt but that they and the Loriyān Tangai fragment came from one and the same atelier, and it is highly probable that the atelier was in the Sanghao-Nathu district. Fig. 113, which is now in the Lahore Museum, is a rectangular panel, picturing the miracle of the black snake at Rājagṛiha. The story was that a wealthy miser of Rājagṛiha buried his treasure in his garden. After death he turned into a black snake in order to guard it, and in that form terrorized the neighbourhood. At the request of King Bimbisāra the Buddha subdued the snake, which forthwith crept into his begging-bowl. In the centre of this relief stands the thick-set, stocky figure of the Buddha, holding his begging-bowl in his hand with the snake coiled inside it. Below, is a clump of lotuses growing from a small patch of water, and near by stands Bimbisāra, gazing reverently at the snake. At the Buddha's left side is the Vajrapāṇi—a bearded figure armed with a sword —and round about are courtiers and attendants, four on one side and four on the other. Apart from the bearded Vajrapāṇi there are two distinct types of faces in this relief, namely, a thinnish type with long nose and lips rising at the corners, as seen in the faces of the king and the courtier immediately above him, and a much fuller type with short nose, rounded cheeks and softer mouth, as seen in the Buddha and the two attendant figures next to him. These two facial types are characteristic of all the reliefs belonging to this small group, and so, too, are the elaborate head-dresses of the male and female figures. In point of style and workmanship the reliefs show some disparity, enough at least to prove that they are not all by the same hand. None of them, however, is of a high order. Indeed, the impression they convey is that they are the work of indifferent copyists. As to their date, certain early features, like the elaborate head-dresses, the type of the Buddha in fig. 113 and the heavy leaf canopy in *A.M.I.* No. 136, might suggest relegating the group to the Early phase of the Maturity Period, but the stylized grouping of the figures and the modelling of some of them individually (e.g. the *devas* squatting on the acanthus capitals in *A.M.I.* No. 97) point rather to the Later phase. Probably we shall be near the truth if we place them at the very beginning of that phase.

With fig. 114 we return to the main current of Gandhāra art. This small upright panel (*urdhvapatta*) of unknown provenance is now in the Lahore Museum. The main subject, illustrated in the lowest register, is Gautama's Flight from the City. In the centre, unhappily much mutilated, the Bodhisattva is shown *de face* riding out of Kapilavastu, on his horse Kaṇṭhaka, and beside him, on his left, is the lithe and elegant figure of his groom Chandaka, holding the royal umbrella over his master's head. On the Bodhisattva's right is Māra, the Evil One, who tried in vain to deflect the future Buddha from his purpose by offering him the sovereignty of the world. The identity of the other figures is less certain but the much defaced female on the extreme right is probably the city-goddess of Kapilavastu lamenting over the Bodhisattva's departure, while the princely figure next to her may well be Indra.

In the two upper registers are abbreviated clichés of well-known scenes which preceded the Flight. In the middle one the Bodhisattva is shown seated on the side of a couch in the pose normally associated with the 'Sleeping Women' scene. On his right are his horse and groom, waiting for him to mount; on his left, a very alert guard, grasping a spear. At the top, the 'Life of Pleasure' seems to be symbolized by the royal couple seated side by side on a couch and two of their attendants apparently overcome by sleep or drink.

The school to which this sculpture belonged had reached its zenith during the first phase of the Maturity Period, and the decline which it had since suffered can be appreciated by comparing this slab with, for example, fig. 92 above. The earlier relief, as we have seen, impresses us with the creative artistry of its author. The grouping, though on traditional lines, is well thought out, the individual figures carefully executed, and a few of them remarkably graceful. In the later relief, the crowd of figures in the lowest tier, though modelled with much skill and charm, are of more conventional types and lose their individual significance by being so closely packed together—a feature which is probably due to increasing Indian influence. For the rest, the poor quality both of the design as a whole and of the figural modelling, seems to betray a marked lack of ability on the part of the sculptor.

One of the best known and most striking examples of Gandhāra art is a relief of phyllite in the Calcutta Museum which depicts the episodes of the White dog barking at the Buddha and of the Buddha exhibiting the serpent to the Kāśyapa brothers (fig. 115). The first of these episodes occurred when the Buddha was paying a call on a householder named Śuka in the neighbourhood of Śrāvastī. Śuka himself chanced to be out, and his dog, which was eating its food on a couch, barked furiously at the visitor. The Buddha bade it be quiet and told it that it was because it had been so rich in a former life that it had now been brought to its present grievous state. Whereupon the dog crept disconsolate into a corner. When Śuka returned and asked the meaning of it all, the Buddha explained that the dog had been Śuka's own father in his previous life, and bade Śuka ask the dog where his father's treasure had been hidden before he died. Śuka obeyed, and thereupon the dog crawled beneath the couch and began to scratch at the floor, and, sure enough, when they dug there, they found the treasure. This episode occupies the left end of the relief and comprises four figures, namely, the Buddha, a much defaced figure of the Vajrapāṇi behind him, the dog barking on a couch, and another partly defaced figure on the farther side of the couch, presumably intended for Śuka. But the dog and couch alone would have been quite enough for a Buddhist to identify the scene.

The second episode, to the right of the foregoing, took place when the Buddha was staying with the Kāśyapa brothers in their hermitage at Uruvilvā. In a corner of the hermitage was a fire-temple in which there dwelt at the time of the Buddha's visit a particularly fierce and venomous snake, a terror to all around. With the reluctant consent of the Kāśyapas, the Buddha took up his abode in the temple, and the snake, cowed into submission by the mere effulgence of his being, crept meekly into his begging-bowl. In our relief the Buddha is shown holding up the begging-bowl and the snake inside it for the Kāśyapas to see. Beside him is the Vajrapāṇi, here a naked figure, and in front the three Kāśyapas, recognizable at once by the cut of their garments falling in a V-shape below the knees. Above, between the Buddha and the Kāśyapas appears the upper part of a youthful *deva* with long hair and the pretty type of girlish face which is so characteristic of this period. At the right end of the slab is part of a third group illustrating another episode, which owing to the mutilation of the stone cannot now be identified. In order to make it clear that he was depicting three separate scenes the artist has resorted to the usual device of repeating the figure of the Buddha and his attendant Vajrapāṇi in each one of them. But for this it might have been hard to distinguish between the scenes, since the figures are disposed in an unbroken line across the face of the panel. This was, of course, the Greek method which we have already encountered in a number of earlier reliefs (figs. 40–50), and besides this feature there is much else in this relief to remind us of Hellenistic work. But we have only to compare it with, for example, fig. 41, to realize what a very artificial and mimetic thing the Hellenism of Gandhāra art had become in the intervening century. In the earlier relief, the figures, though strung out in semi-isolation and looking in consequence a little self-conscious, are nevertheless natural and unaffected, each with a convincing personality of its own. Their charm lies in their very simplicity and moderation. By contrast, the later relief appears over-stylized and conventional, Greek in form but not in feeling. Indeed, the sculptor seems bent on showing off his cleverness (which is exceptional) in the modelling of the nude and in the effective display of drapery. It is all very praiseworthy, but all rather overdone. Despite their elegance and vitality, his figures lack altogether the engaging charm of the earlier ones.

The one unmutilated head of the *deva* in the background belongs to a type that became very familiar in the latter part of the second century A.D. but is quite unlike any *deva* of the preceding century. Were there still any likelihood of this relief being confused (as it used to be) with the earlier work, this head alone would suffice to settle the question. The conventional beauty and superb craftsmanship that distinguish this sculpture are characteristic of a great variety of other sculptures referable to the same age, including many fine architectural pieces and a great array of Buddha and Bodhisattva statues (e.g. figs. 128, 129, 138, 139, 140, 142, etc.).

The four following pieces, figs. 116–19, afford striking illustrations of the growing formality and stylization which marked the work of this period and of the increasing popularity of the pretty-faced *devas*. Fig. 116 is an upright panel (*urdhvapatta*), about 24 in. high, of greyish-white micaceous schist, which came originally from Jamāl-Garhī and is now in the Calcutta Museum. It depicts three scenes from the story of Nanda, half-brother of the Buddha. Of the bottom one, nothing is now left except four pretty heads of *devas* looking on while Nanda is being enticed from his home by the Buddha. This part of the story is told in fig. 121, where Nanda is shown leaving his lovely wife and starting out, with the Buddha's begging-bowl in hand, to accompany him back to his monastery. But, alas, for Nanda! No sooner had they arrived there than Nanda, much against his will, had his head shaved by the monks' barber and was forthwith ordained into the Order. This is the scene depicted in the middle panel where the barber is in the act of shaving Nanda, while the Buddha pours out the ceremonial water. At the Buddha's right shoulder stands the Vajrapāṇi with beard carefully curled in the fashion of the time; and gazing down benignly on the scene are the angelic faces of four *devas* similar to those in the panel below. From then on Nanda was kept an unwilling prisoner in the monastery, and the top panel depicts one of his many attempts to escape. On this occasion he had been left in sole charge of the monastery, with instructions from the Buddha to close all the cell doors before going out. This he tried to do, but had no sooner shut one door than another flew open. So at last he gave up trying and set out to return to his home. But in vain; for as he made his way stealthily through a wood, the Buddha suddenly appeared, advancing towards him; and when Nanda tried to hide behind a tree, the tree rose into the air, leaving him face to face with the Master, who promptly marched him back to the monastery. The story, as told in the relief, is unmistakable. First, on the extreme right, the figure of Nanda locking one of the monastery doors; then the same figure kneeling at the feet of the Buddha, with the tree suspended in the air above his head, while the Vajrapāṇi and other figures stand by, and the celestials look on from above.

Looking at the carefully regimented and highly stylized figures of this and the two following pieces, one cannot but admire their suave and elegant beauty and the exquisite delicacy of the carving. But one misses the freshness and originality of the older work: the power to give life and dramatic cohesion to a scene apart from its merely mechanical structure. The charm of these sculptures might fitly be compared with that of ornamental flower-beds which require much skill and good taste on the part of the gardener, but no very high degree of creative talent.

The three reliefs which follow (figs. 117–19) all come from Loriyān Tangai and are made of the same micaceous schist as the foregoing. The subject of fig. 117 is the Buddha preaching his First Sermon in the Deer Park at Sārnāth. It is the same subject as that depicted in fig. 4, and probably also in fig. 59, but in fig. 4, which belongs to the Early Indian School, there is only a wheel set on the top of a column to symbolize the 'Wheel of the Law' (*dharmacakra*) which, in Buddhist parlance, the Teacher then for the first time set in motion; and below it some deer to symbolize the Deer Park. In this Gandhāran relief (fig. 117) the same symbols are repeated, but the centre of the picture is occupied by the Teacher himself seated on a grass-strewn throne beneath a mango canopy. On his right and left are Kauṇḍinya and his companions—the Band of Five—listening to his immortal words, and beyond them, in symmetrical array, a troupe of celestial figures, with the ever-faithful Vajrapāṇi in the background. Note the strongly characterized face of Kauṇḍinya, seated next to the Buddha on his right, which contrasts so sharply with the doll-like countenances of the *devas*, all fashioned in one mould. These neat and elegant celestials, substantially smaller in stature than the monks, are, as already noted, an outstanding feature of this period. On the other hand, the portrait-like head of Kauṇḍinya calls vividly to mind the features of the monks in fig. 59. As both these reliefs emanate from Loriyān Tangai and both are made of the same stone, it seems likely that, despite their great difference in age, they may have been products of the same art school.

The elaborate composition in fig. 118 depicts the familiar scene of Indra's visit to the Buddha at the Indraśaila cave. Within the cave the Buddha is seated in meditation, while tongues of flame, kindled by the radiance of his being, lick the walls around. Beneath him, a lion and a wild pig (?) peer meekly from their lairs among the rocks, and not far away are a deer and a wild sheep besides monkeys, peacocks and other wild animals, all serving to proclaim not only the wildness of the spot but the peace that descends on all nature in the presence of the Blessed One. Outside the cave, Indra, distinguished by his tall hat, approaches reverently from the Buddha's left, and opposite to him, on the Buddha's right, is the harpist Pañcaśikha. To complete the picture, two tree-spirits, ensconced in the foliage of their trees, and a multitude of heavenly beings are casting flowers and paying homage to the Buddha. In conformity with the dictates of long-established tradition, the forms and features of the *devas* are all of one type. As we saw in connexion with fig. 7, this tradition was observed by sculptors of the Early Indian School as far back as the first century B.C., but although the tradition had been maintained since then, the type itself of these heavenly beings had undergone significant changes in the meantime. Thus, the *devas* who compose the heavenly host in the scene of Māra's defeat in fig. 7, are neither very young nor very comely. Clean-shaven and with fat cheeks and well-nourished bodies, they are merely replicas of the earthly princes and nobles figured in other scenes on the same gateways, and they are dressed in the same attire. This Indian type was sometimes reproduced by the sculptors of Gandhāra, but during the Adolescent Period the *devas* usually wore moustaches and had younger and more forceful expressions (e.g. figs. 59, 60, 62, 67). This moustached type lasted on, along with the moustached type of the Buddha, into the Early Maturity Period, but I cannot recall any later examples than figs. 96, 97. At that time youthful and comely faces, alike for mortals and immortals, were already becoming the fashion. Thus in fig. 84 the god Indra has a particularly girlish and attractive face, and in fig. 87 not only the *devas* but the aged and dying Buddha himself have the same pleasant, half-smiling features. Another striking example is furnished by fig. 107, where the two *devas* at the top, haloed and richly attired, have just the same effeminate countenances as the pair of diving 'angels' (a wholly different class of being) who, like them, are showering flowers on the Buddha. By the time fig. 118 was carved, the number of celestials crowding the scene had much increased, and the multiplicity of similar faces could not but have a monotonous effect. Yet, with all their shortcomings, there is much in these and other sculptures of the same School to compel our admiration. For they have a quiet, gentle melody of their own, and they breathe an air of peace and happiness and goodwill that is the soul of Buddhism. What more could a good Buddhist ask for?

In the last of these examples (fig. 119), which is the latest of the four, we see the same formality in the disposition of the figures, the same sort of prettiness in the faces of the *devas* and *devīs*. Indeed, the *devī* at the back of the horse's head, who is evidently intended for the city-goddess of Kapilavastu (*nagara-devatā*), must be considered beautiful by any standard. But for the most part the figures are like puppets, with heads too big for their bodies, and movements that are stiff and ungainly. The episode here recounted is the same as that in fig. 114, the flight of the Bodhisattva from Kapilavastu, but instead of the young prince and his horse being shown from the front, they are shown in profile, moving from right to left. In the earlier relief the two *yakshas* supporting the horse's feet are defaced; but here they are well preserved, and so, too, are the other actors in the scene, namely Chandaka the groom, who stands behind the horse holding the royal umbrella over his master, and above him, in the background, the Vajrapāṇi; while in front of the horse is Māra, bow in hand, and at his back the haloed figure of Indra (cf. fig. 114 above).

The foregoing relief is referable to the close of the Later Maturity Period, in the early part of the third century A.D. Of about the same age, but entirely different in style, is fig. 120, a relief of phyllite stone from Mamāne-Dheṛī, near Chārsada, which, like fig. 118, features Indra's visit to the Buddha in the Indraśaila cave. If we compare the two panels, we see at once how widely they differ in detail and in the quality of their artistry. Thus we note that the walls of the cave, which in fig. 118 were flaming with the effulgence of the Buddha's person, present a hard, almost bare outline in fig. 120; that the Buddha himself is seated on a throne in the former, on the ground in the latter; that the wild animals beneath the front of the cave in the former are replaced by a line of figures in the latter; that Indra is represented in person in the former, by his elephant Airāvata in the latter; and that, whereas in the former the wild and rocky jungle round the cave, with its birds and animals, and adoring *devas* and *devīs* and tree-spirits, is shown in one unbroken array, in the latter the scene is parcelled out by narrow ledges into a number of compartments with a small group of figures in each. We note, too, that the *devas* and *devīs* in fig. 120 are not distinguished by the stereotype prettiness of feature that characterizes them in fig. 118; and that the execution, particularly of the draperies, in fig. 120 falls far short of that in fig. 118. That these points of difference are not attributable to the personal idiosyncrasies of the artist of the later sculpture, but to the traditions of his school, is proved by another and earlier relief from the Dharmarājikā at Taxila[1] which displays the same traditional features but a livelier and more naturalistic way of handling them. In choosing fig. 120 for illustration in preference to this earlier and more attractive piece from the Dharmarājikā I was influenced by the fact that it bears on its base a Kharoshṭhī inscription dated in the year 87 of the Kanishka era. According to the now generally accepted chronology of this period, this date falls within a few years of A.D. 224 and it thus confirms the date of this sculpture arrived at on stylistic grounds (cf. *C.I.I.* vol. II, p. 171, and pl. 34).

Love of the decorative was, and still is, inherent in the Indian temperament, and in the Early Indian School it was constantly asserting itself in one direction or another. Thus, among the few selected examples of the Sāñchī sculptures illustrated in figs. 1–12 we drew attention to the decorative design of the lotus plant in fig. 2 and to the decorative handling of the fleeing hosts of Māra in fig. 7. This instinctive feeling for the decorative which is a hall-mark of Indian art at all ages becomes increasingly apparent in the art of Gandhāra in the latter part of the second century A.D., and there can be little doubt that this spread of Indian influence resulted from the closer contacts between India and Gandhāra after the extension of Kushān rule over Central India and Hindustān. The first effect of this influence was to impart a certain quiet charm to

[1] Cf. *Taxila*, vol. II, pp. 718–19, no. 124, and vol. III, pl. 221.

compositions which were tending to become stilted and formal—such compositions, I mean, as those illustrated in figs. 117 and 118. But this initial charm soon wore thin, for though the sculptors of Gandhāra might imitate with some success the superficial embellishments of Indian art, they could not absorb the innate genius of the Indian for the decorative, and so, in the long run, Indian influence led to little more than the display of multiple figures in formal, sometimes geometric, array, or to conventional and sterile designs in which architecture played an increasingly dominant part.

The employment of architecture as a setting for dramatic scenes was, of course, familiar in earlier Gandhāra art, but in fig. 121 the emphasis laid on the setting is out of all proportion to the scene as a whole. This relief, which I judge to date from the Second Maturity Period, comes from Haḍḍa in Southern Afghānistān and is made of the fine limestone found in that region. Its subject is the first or 'Enticement' scene in the Conversion of Nanda, half-brother of the Buddha, the later scenes of which we have already encountered in fig. 116. Nanda is here shown as he leaves the chamber of his bride carrying the Buddha's begging-bowl; to the left he is again shown tendering the bowl to the Buddha, who refuses to take it, thus inducing the prince to return with him to his monastery, where, despite his protestations, he is forthwith shaved and ordained. The figures in the gallery above are the same as those at the top of the lowest panel of fig. 116, namely the *devas* and *devīs* witnessing the Buddha's stratagem from aloft. In this relief the architecture is still an integral part of the scene, providing an imaginative and fanciful representation of the prince's palace. But it is much overdone in relation to the rest of the picture, and is already paving the way for the use of architecture as the principal factor in compositions of an outstandingly decorative character, countless examples of which are to be seen among the Early Indian sculptures of Bhārhut, Bodh-Gayā, Sāñchī and Mathurā. This further stage is well illustrated in figs. 122 and 123, the former from Loriyān Tangai, the latter of schist from Muhammad Nāri. The subject of both pieces is the same as that illustrated in fig. 100, namely, the Miracle of Śrāvastī, when, in order to convert the unbelievers, the Buddha sat preaching in mid-air on a lotus provided by the two Nāga kings, Nanda and Upananda, and caused unending replicas of himself to appear stretching up to

Heaven. The canopy above his head was provided by a mango-tree which he caused to grow miraculously from a seed. It is recorded that he preached in mid-air with flames issuing from his shoulders and a stream of water from his feet, and it is also recorded that a special pavilion for the performance of the miracle (*prātihārya-maṇḍapa*) was built by King Prasenajit. This most wonderful of all miracles was a specially favourite theme at this period, and in the normal versions some characteristic details are shown by which the miracle can at once be identified: the lotus, for example, and the Nāga-rājas who produced it, or the replicas of the Buddha imaged in mid-air, or the flames issuing from his head and the water flowing from his feet. But in fig. 122 the only features that remotely connect it with the great miracle are the border of conventional lotus leaves fringing the edge of the stool on which the Buddha is seated and the architectural setting which presumably represents the pavilion built by King Prasenajit. For the rest, it is a matter of guesswork to identify the scene or the actors in it. Indeed, it is not at the performance of the Śrāvastī Miracle that we are invited to wonder so much as at a highly decorative composition in which the figures are of little more consequence than the finely carved columns and balconies, the amorini and garland design adorning the plinth, and the miniature shrines and false windows that crown the roof.

In fig. 123, another relief referable to the close of this Later Maturity Period, the decorative scheme is much the same, but the architectural features are more fanciful and ornate, and the artist has paid closer attention to the canonical features of the miracle, so that it can be identified at a glance. Thus the lotus whereon the Buddha is seated is a more realistic plant which at once catches the eye; and two of the re-duplicated images are shown beneath the small arches on either side of the Buddha's head. This representation of the Grand Miracle, it should be noted, is confined to the middle band of the relief, between which and the upper and lower bands there appears to be no more than a decorative, tactile connexion. Of the two small scenes in the false window above the Buddha's head, the lower is recognizable as the 'Sleep of the Women', the upper as the 'Flight of the Bodhisattva from Kapilavastu'. In the miniature shrines to right and left are seated Bodhisattva figures with an attendant standing on either side. The group at the bottom of the panel is made up of the last Buddha (Śākyamuni) in the centre, with the six previous Buddhas and the future Buddha (Maitreya) on his right and left, and beyond them figures of devotees, including perhaps the donor or donors. The late date of this carving is confirmed by many minor details, both figural and architectural, among them the dressing of Śākyamuni's hair in tight ringlets and the designs of the *yaksha*-supported pillars in the middle band.

By way of contrast with these typical examples of the architectural style, I have appended two more reliefs of the Grand Miracle executed in the more usual style of the period (figs. 124 and 125). Both reliefs are carved out of ordinary phyllite-stone and are characteristic of Gandhāra sculpture towards the end of the second century A.D., when art had become smug and complacent, and even craftsmanship was already on the wane. From an iconographic point of view these two reliefs are also instructive. Fig. 124 shows Śākyamuni seated on a lotus beneath a canopy provided by the miraculous mango tree. Of the four attendant figures the pair at the back are to be identified clearly as Indra and Brahmā, Indra by his high hat and the *vajra* he is carrying; Brahmā by his head-dress and the flask in his left hand. It follows, then, that the Bodhisattva on the Buddha's left, who is likewise carrying a flask, must be Maitreya, the future Buddha, while the one on his right is presumably Mañjuśrī or Avalokiteśvara.

In fig. 125 the figure of Indra is missing, owing to a break in the stone, but the other three attendant figures correspond to those in fig. 124. Two items of this relief that deserve notice are the Nāga elephants supporting the lotus on which the Buddha is seated and the highly elaborated design of the miraculous mango canopy above the Buddha's head. Emerging from the cluster of leaves in this canopy are little tree-fairies, one about to crown the Buddha with a flowery wreath, two with garlands in their hands, and two in attitudes of adoration. In another example of the same kind of canopy (fig. 126) the wreath is borne by two fairies, while above them is another carrying a garland. The fairies in this relief, but not in fig. 125, are provided with *ushṇīshas* and haloes. That the glorification of the Buddha in these reliefs was inspired by the familiar apotheosis crowning-scenes of Hellenistic art admits of no doubt, but it should also be observed that the miraculous canopy and its tree-spirits are thoroughly Indian while the manner of depicting them is in the best tradition of Gandhāra art at this period. Another good example of the decorative tendency in some of the sculptures of this period is afforded by a comparison of figs. 127–9. All three of these belong to the Later Maturity Period and all depict the same event, namely, the death (*Mahāparinirvāṇa*) of the Buddha. The first of the three, which comes from the Swāt Valley and is now in the Calcutta Museum, might at first sight be thought to be a work of the Adolescent Period. Compare it, for example, with fig. 68, and note the wild sorrow in the faces of the Malla chiefs behind the bier, the grief-stricken figure of Mahākāśyapa at the feet of the Buddha, and the fantastic carvings on the legs of the bier. In spite of the air of artificiality which pervades the whole, these features are more nearly akin to work of the previous century than to that exemplified in figs. 128 and 129. But when we look at the statue-like figure of the dying Buddha himself and at the *deva* behind him with his hand raised in salute, we see at once that the relief could not possibly be earlier than the Later Maturity Period. The fact is that this is an example (of which there are not a few in Gandhāra art) of archaistic work, i.e. of work which was copied from older models. But in this case the sculptor has copied his prototype in part only, and has then lapsed into the smooth, pretty, and conventional style of his own day.

The next relief (fig. 128) which also comes from Swāt[1] and is now in the Calcutta Museum, is of a very different style. The principle underlying its composition is much the same as that of figs. 127 and 129, but here the decorative element has been accentuated by increasing the number of figures and so arranging them that they produce a tapestry-like pattern of light and dark such as we are familiar with in reliefs of the Sāñchī gateways (cf. figs. 7 and 10*b*, above), though in the earlier work the effect is more natural and spontaneous. That fig. 128 dates from the Later Maturity Period there can be no question. It is patent in every detail: in the border of sea monsters ridden by Amorini; in the line of floating 'angels' above the assemblage; in the smooth girlish faces of the celestials showering down their flowers and glorifying the Blessed One; in the statue-like figure on the couch, and in the exquisitely fine carving of the figures—carving such as we have already remarked on the canopies of figs. 125 and 126 and that we shall meet again in many of the contemporary images and architectural members (e.g. figs. 137–9 and 145–7). Such miniature-like carving is more suited to ivory than to stone and it

[1] M. Foucher ascribes this to Loriyān Tangai, but that seems to be an error.

was in all probability imitated from ivory work of the period. As to the actors in this scene, note the unusual appearance and position of the bearded Vajrapāṇi seated beside Subhadra, the Buddha's last convert, in front of the couch, and note the tall monk holding a fly-whisk at the Buddha's head, whom Foucher identifies with Upavāna. The monk holding a staff on the extreme left is no doubt Mahākāśyapa, and the nude figure beside him the Ājīvika who had given him the news of the Buddha's death. The monk who has fallen on his knees at the foot of the couch is presumably Ānanda, and the one raising him from the ground Anuruddha. The tall princely-looking couple on the extreme right must, I think, be Indra and his consort, not Malla nobles as Foucher was inclined to think. This I infer from the *vajra* carried by the male figure in his left hand, a detail which Foucher's photograph probably failed to disclose.

Of fig. 129, which depicts the same scene, little need be said. It is a crude, commonplace piece of work referable to the closing years of the Later Maturity Period and gives us the measure of the degeneration which was taking place in the output of many of the Gandhāra ateliers at this time, though other ateliers were still maintaining a somewhat higher level. And here we may profitably pause for a moment to look back at the earlier representations of the *Parinirvāṇa* illustrated above in figs. 68, 72, 87, 127 and 128, and observe how in the century and more that intervened between the first and last of this series Gandhāra sculpture lost, step by step, its old virile spirit and its power of imaginative expression. Contemplating fig. 72, we are immediately conscious of the dramatic sense of the artist, of the 'rapture of repose' portrayed in the lifeless features of the Blessed One, of the crushing sorrow in the tearful faces of the Vajrapāṇi and the monks in the foreground, of the despair of the Malla chiefs in the background, and of the contrasting impassivity of the *deva* at their side. But when we turn to fig. 129, what do we see? On the bed in the centre a figure that looks for all the world like a stone image fallen on its side—and round about the bier a group of puppet-like figures, with smooth, boyish faces as plump and fatuous as that of the corpse itself and indistinguishable from it or from one another. We can recognize the Vajrapāṇi by the *vajra* in his hand, and Mahākāśyapa by the nude ascetic at his side. Whether the other figures are meant to be celestials or Malla chiefs, it would be hard to say.

Finally, as a tail-piece to this chapter, I have added fig. 130, as another example of the low level to which much Gandhāra sculpture had sunk by the early part of the third century A.D. The scene is one from the Viśvantara Jātaka, with which we have already made acquaintance in fig. 6. It shows the Bodhisattva in the royal chariot with his wife and two children in the act of giving away his purse to the Brāhman. There is a lively fancy in the half-comic figure of the fat, repulsive-looking Brāhman, and there is decorative value in the stylish design of the horses and chariot. But at best it is a crude and artificial piece of work, the very antithesis of the natural, picturesque portrayal of the same Jātaka by an artist of the Early Indian School at Sāñchī (fig. 6).

CHAPTER II

# LATER MATURITY PERIOD: IMAGES AND DECORATIVE CARVINGS

(FIGS. 131–51)

No form of art is so conservative as sacred art, and nothing in that art more conservative than the cult image. This is true of the sacred art of all ages and in all parts of the world, and the Graeco-Buddhist art of Gandhāra was no exception to the rule. But even in images of the Buddha and of the Bodhisattvas changes and modifications are visible which after the fixation of the orthodox types continue to reflect the changing fashions. Such changes are well exemplified in fig. 131. Compare it, for example, with fig. 111, which dates from the Early Maturity Period. Anyone not very familiar with Gandhāra art might readily take these two statues to be of the same age and school, but that fig. 131 in reality is referable to a substantially later period than fig. 111 is clear from several features; for, whereas the Buddha in fig. 111 is wearing a moustache and has his eyes wide open and his hair taken back from the forehead over the *ushṇīsha*, in fig. 131 he has no moustache, the eyes are half-closed and the hair is dressed in tight little ringlets. Apart, too, from these significant features, there is a notable difference in the general style of the two statues, that of fig. 111 being free and unconstrained—the work of a sculptor with an innate sense for simple rhythmic form; while that of fig. 131 is tight, laboured and self-conscious—the work of a craftsman rather than an artist, who, like many of his contemporaries, was showing off his skill in the mechanical excellence and precision of his carving. Should any doubt still exist as to the age of this image, it is completely set at rest by the figural relief adorning its base. Such figural reliefs on the pedestals of statues did not come into fashion until the middle of the second century A.D., and to judge by its style this particular relief can hardly be earlier than the last quarter of that century.

Only in one particular, namely in the facial features, does this image display any real individuality. There is nothing, of course, exceptional in the half-closed eyes, with their suggestion of other-worldliness, which convention now required, but there is something definitely exceptional in the half-sulky and very undistinguished expression on the face, very different from the calm and placid look which usually characterizes the Buddha's images of this period and which is strikingly exemplified in the figures that follow (figs. 132–5). Of these, fig. 132 has been much publicized. Foucher, who in my view exaggerated its merits, wrote of it as 'the most beautiful, and probably also the most ancient of the Buddhas, which it has ever been granted to me to encounter',[1] and he assigned it to the first century B.C., that is, to a date some two centuries earlier than the actual one. Unquestionably the shapely, graceful head of this image, with its firmly modelled features and subtle smile, is a fine bit of work. But it cannot be pretended that there is anything particularly spiritual in its expression, nor, as regards the rest of the statue, does it show any superiority over many other images of this period, either in the general proportions of the figure or in the technical skill displayed in the draping and finishing of the monk's robe. Indeed, the modelling of the ankles and feet is more than usually clumsy, though this is a blemish shared by many otherwise commendable statues both of this and earlier periods.

In the second volume of *L'art gréco-bouddhique du Gandhāra*, M. Foucher gives the place of honour in the frontispiece to another Buddha statue of the same type and no doubt from the same atelier as fig. 132, but the work of a less gifted sculptor. Luckily this statue, which was found at Chārsada and is now in the Lahore Museum, has its base adorned with a figural bas-relief identical in style with the one on fig. 131, and, like it, referable to the latter part of the second century A.D., thus confirming the date already arrived at on other grounds.

Among the countless images of the Buddha dating from this period there were, needless to say, many differing varieties produced by the many ateliers in Gandhāra. To the two examples of these varieties described above space allows me to add only three more (figs. 133–6). One of them is the gentle, benevolent, homely-looking figure illustrated in fig. 133, where the Buddha is shown with three of the Kāśyapa brothers, who can be recognized, as in fig. 115, by the pointed garment (here reaching to the ground) of the figure on the right. In this statue

[1] *Beginnings of Buddhist Art*, trans. by L. A. Thomas and F. W. Thomas, p. 119 and pl. XI, 2.

observe that the hair is taken back from the forehead over the *ushṇīsha*, as in the older statues and as in figs. 134 and 135; and observe, too, the character of the scroll pattern on the base of this statue which is found on other pieces of the same period.

Of a wholly different character and of a somewhat later date are the two images, one standing and the other seated, illustrated in figs. 134 and 135. With their well-rounded forms and smooth, pretty faces, these uninspired images fall into line with the conventional *devas* and *devīs* so peculiarly characteristic of this period, but it goes without saying that cult images of this kind, which are fashioned in accordance with the strict canonical rules of the Church, are inevitably more set and formal in their expression than other figures, whether celestial or terrestrial, executed by the same artist. The standing image has lost its base, but the line of *Dhyāni*-Buddhas seated under leafy canopies and supported by worshippers which adorns the base of the seated image (fig. 135) is a sure proof of its late date.

By the side of the broad and fleshy frames of the two foregoing images, fig. 136, with its slender torso, relatively narrow shoulders and demure-looking countenance, presents an almost effeminate appearance. Its date must lie very near to the close of the Later Maturity Period, between about A.D. 220 and 230. Evidence of this late date is afforded by the squarish shape of the projecting knees, which at this time was becoming more and more marked, but still more by the figures on the base, which, instead of forming a separate panel as in figs. 131 or 135, now play their part directly in front of the drapery of the throne itself as if an integral part of it. This method of treating subsidiary reliefs is an indubitable sign of their late date.

When we turn from the Buddha to the Bodhisattva images, we are at once struck by the stylishness and superlatively fine workmanship which distinguish the vast majority of the latter. Among the most noteworthy types is that represented by figs. 137 and 138, the former a statue of Maitreya from the Mohṛā Morādu Monastery at Taxila, the latter a fragment only which was at one time in the Guides' Mess at Mardān. All the Bodhisattvas are princely figures, attired in princely robes and wearing a wealth of jewellery shown in meticulous detail. But in the figures of this particular group there is a certain dandyism and swagger which shows itself not only in their personal bearing and waved moustaches, but in the cut of their dress and in the pointed, well-folded hems of their skirts. Fig. 138 comprises only the head and shoulders, but I have thought it worth including it here because it shows up so clearly the details of the ornaments and the beauty of the chiselling, as clean-cut and precise as could be found in any school of sculpture, East or West.

Another group of these images of a notably different style is represented by figs. 139 and 140, the former from Sahrī-Bahlol and now in the Peshāwar Museum, the latter in the Lahore Museum. This group was a large one and survived well on into the third century, showing increasing evidence of deterioration up to the last. All wear the same princely attire and ornaments, but their demeanour is simple and unassuming, without affectation or dandyism. One of the earliest and best is fig. 139, which, like so many cult statues of this period, represents the Bodhisattva Maitreya, as a symbol of whom he holds a flask (*kamaṇḍalu*) in his left hand. The eyes, like those of the Buddha, are half-closed, the moustache small and unobtrusive, the torso relatively slim and shapely. Evidence of date is furnished by the drapery, and particularly by the pleated and scalloped border of the skirt, and still more precisely by the figural relief on the pedestal, of which there are many close parallels.

Of the melancholy process of decline through which this group of images passed towards the close of this period dozens of examples might be cited. We must content ourselves with one (fig. 140). In this example, the essential traits are virtually the same: the half-closed eyes, the turbanless head, the ostentatious jewellery, the *kamaṇḍalu*, and the drapery; but the face is flabby and undistinguished, the torso fat and heavy, the legs and arms wooden, the drapery less graceful than it had been. And observe that the halo is now rimmed with triangular rays, that there is a second underskirt beneath the normal one, and that the relief on the pedestal (the worship of the Buddha's bowl) also gives the measure of decaying art.

Of yet another style and certainly of earlier date than the last is the image of Siddhārtha meditating in the shade of the Jambu tree at the Ploughing Festival (fig. 141). The festival is represented on the face of the pedestal by a ploughman and his yoke of oxen on the right, with three robed figures at prayer in front of an incense burner to the left. The intimate connexion between this panel and the Bodhisattva is shown by the way the sculptor has allowed the drapery to fall over the top of the panel: as if making it an integral part of itself. The figure of the young prince is singularly soft and graceful, his expression gentle and sorrowing as befitted the occasion. Indeed, in this statue there is a hint of deeper feeling which is unusual at this time. Yet no one familiar with Gandhāra sculpture could make the mistake of relegating it to any other period than the latter part of the Later Maturity Period. This date is attested not only by the very 'plastic' quality of the modelling and the fine finish of the details, but also by the character of the pedestal relief and by the treatment of the drapery folds in front of the left leg, which by a false mannerism of the time are shown out of the vertical (cf. fig. 143 below).

The queer, gnome-like Maitreya reproduced in fig. 142 is said by Major Cole to have come from Miyān Khān, but the Calcutta Museum Catalogue ascribes it to the Upper Monastery at Nathu.[1] Whichever is correct, it seems not unlikely that it is a very late effort from one of the Nathu-Sanghao ateliers. Its lateness alone, however, would obviously not account for its strange, almost elfish appearance or the utter gracelessness of its form. In this statue note that the halo is rayed and the hair bound round the *ushṇīsha* in the same way as in fig. 140, but that its waved moustache and debonair look are reminiscent rather of figs. 137 and 138, while the eyelids have the rare distinction of being almost wide open. A feature which it shares with some other very late images is the peculiar frilling round the scalloped hem of the skirt. The lotus base may signify that the Bodhisattva is conceived of as still in the Tushita heaven, but its meaning is not certain.

Besides these cult statues of the Buddha and Bodhisattvas, there are many other images which equally well reflect the changing character of Gandhāra sculpture during this period. Two such are the figures of Pāñcika, the genius of riches, and his consort Hāritī illustrated in figs. 143 and 144. For many years fig. 143, which is in the Lahore Museum, was called a Scythian Chief. Later, it was identified with Kubera, Guardian of the Northern Quarter and king of the Yakshas. It was left to M. Foucher to identify it more precisely with Kubera's general, Pāñcika, Dispenser of Riches and consort of Hāritī, the goddess of Fertility. The pair were very popular in Gandhāra in the latter part of the second

[[1] Major Cole, in his *Graeco-Buddhist Sculptures from Yusufzai*, pl. 25, also ascribes this sculpture to the Upper Monastery at Nathu. There is therefore no discrepancy as regards its provenance. Ed.]

century, and their statues are many. Fig. 144, which is in the Peshāwar Museum, shows the two deities seated side by side. In both examples Pāñcika's corpulent, well-nourished body and richly jewelled ornaments are appropriate to a god of riches; and the little children clustered about his knees proclaim his intimate connexion with the goddess of Fertility. But in fig. 143 he is more than the personification of material wealth and prosperity. He is also a warrior, commander-in-chief (*senapati*) of Kubera's army, and it is for this reason that the sculptor has placed a spear in his hand and endowed him with such strong, imperious features and a look of fierce determination in his eyes. Altogether, and in spite of his corpulence, this statue of Pāñcika makes a noble, dominating figure, of which the Kushān donor (the one holding a bunch of lotuses in the right-hand bottom corner) may well have been proud. Certainly it is the finest of its kind in Gandhāra. At first sight it is tempting to place this statue near the close of the early phase of the Maturity Period because of its striking originality and individualistic qualities, but the artificial treatment of the drapery falling from the knees in stiff loops and at an impossible angle, and the little figure of the Kushān donor leave no doubt of its later age.

Though not far removed in age from the foregoing, fig. 144 presents a marked contrast in style. Pāñcika, here, has none of the fierceness of the war-god. He is the peace-loving god of wealth and prosperity. His eyes are mild, his features gentle, and he holds no spear in his hand. But the contrast goes deeper than this. For there is no spark of originality in any of the figures of this group. Pāñcika, Hāritī, the cherubic children, even the Bacchic rout on the base—all are typical of the smooth, conventional and well-rounded work that the sculptors of this period were turning out in a ceaseless stream; all finished with exemplary precision, but all dull and uninspired. A feature in which their lack of originality is specially conspicuous is the figures of the children, which are merely stilted replicas of familiar garland-bearing Amorini, like those in figs. 91 and 148, while another is the artificial draping of Pāñcika's skirt over his left knee, which, as in the preceding figure (fig. 143), follows the slope of the leg instead of falling vertically, as the law of gravity requires. It is a blemish common to many sculptures of this period.

In the story of Gandhāra art few figures afford so good an opportunity of comparing the styles of different periods as those of the crouching

Atlants. Turn back, for example, to fig. 52, which is one of the earliest, and remind yourself of the giant strength of this Atlant, of the boldness and simplicity of the modelling and of its freedom from any note of self-consciousness. Then go on to fig. 108 and remark the refined and academic style of the Early Maturity Period, and the conscious effort of the sculptor to be true to his Greek prototype. And now look at the two Atlants illustrated in figs. 145 and 146, both so strikingly typical of the Later Maturity Period. Could anything be more foppish and effeminate than the former, with his carefully curled whiskers, weak mouth and languishing eyes? Or could there be a greater contrast with fig. 52 than the soft angelic form of the latter?

We may conclude this chapter with three more examples (figs. 147–9) selected from decorative pieces of architecture. Particularly attractive is the exquisitely carved Corinthian capital, fig. 147. In stylishness and perfection of technique this capital takes its place beside the finest of the cult statues such as figs. 137 and 138. A happy touch in its design is the little figure of a haloed Bodhisattva emerging from the centre of the acanthus leaves. Much has been written about this type of Gandhāra capital. From the fact that similar figures were introduced into Roman Corinthian capitals for the first time during the reign of Caracalla (A.D. 211–17) the late Vincent Smith inferred that the Gandhāra examples must be later than 217.[1] Vincent Smith's chronology, however, is quite untenable, and there is in fact no justification for supposing that the idea was borrowed from Rome. If there was any copying at all, it is surely more likely to have been done by the West rather than the East since sprightly *devas* and *yakshas* emerging from leaves or flowers had long been a favourite device in the Early Indian School, as witness, for example, the well-known Tree of Life and Fortune on the south jamb of the Western Gateway of the Great Stūpa at Sāñchi which dates from the first century B.C. Obviously this near-at-hand source of Buddhist art was the one from which the idea would be most likely to find its way into the art of Gandhāra.

Though of much the same age as the foregoing, fig. 148 is of a totally different stamp. It is typical of the large group of which the keynotes are a rather smarmy prettiness coupled with a mechanical perfection of

[1] V. A. Smith, 'Graeco-Roman Influence on the Civilization of Ancient India', *J.A.S.B.* LVIII (1889), pp. 107–98.

technique. Notable representatives of this group are figs. 116–19 and 124 among the reliefs, and figs. 134, 135, 139, 140, 141, 144–6 among the statues. With the motif of the wavy garland borne on the shoulders of Amorini or *yakshas* we have already made acquaintance in an earlier example from the Lower Monastery at Nathu (fig. 91), and a comparison of the two gives us a clear idea of the change that came over the spirit of Gandhāra sculpture between the first and second phases of the Maturity Period. While fig. 91 is simple, direct and unpretentious, fig. 148 relies for its charm on its elaboration of decorative detail, its pretty faces and highly-finished workmanship. It is, indeed, about as good a sample of this particular style as could be found. Even when this phase of Gandhāra art was at its zenith such a high standard was exceptional, and in course of time the quality deteriorated more and more. Typical of this large body of inferior carving is the ornamental door-jamb shown in fig. 149, which follows the old Indian pattern but shows little pride of design or workmanship. In this case we are fortunate in having for comparison another door-jamb of the same type (fig. 79) which shows us this same art in its adolescent stage when the Indian and Hellenistic elements were beginning to coalesce. Between the two, Gandhāra art had run most of its course from the first to the third century A.D.

The empire of the great Kushāns came to an end when Vāsudeva was defeated by the Sasānians in the second quarter of the third century A.D., and therewith came also the destruction of the Buddhist monasteries throughout the North-West, evidence of which is furnished by the many small hoards of Vāsudeva's coins found there. They were buried beneath the floors of the monks' cells and not thereafter reclaimed by their owners. From this catastrophe dated also the virtual end of the Gandhāra School of sculpture for which there could henceforth have been little demand. Here and there, no doubt, Buddhist settlements still survived in a shrunken, moribund condition, and descendants of the old sculptors may occasionally have been commissioned to execute such carving as they were capable of. And for the first generation it may be presumed that the standard of their work was maintained at much the same level as it was at the time the monasteries were destroyed; but thereafter, from about A.D. 260 until the come-back of the Kidāra Kushāns four generations later, nothing seems to have been left of the old-time artistry and little of the old-time skill in craftsmanship. Two samples will suffice to make my meaning clear (figs. 150–1). Fig. 150 is a small panel which was purchased near Sahrī-Bahlol and is now in the Peshāwar Museum. It is said to be of steatite and to have come from Afrido-Dheṛī. The subjects depicted are: above, the 'Presentation of the four bowls'; below, the Death Scene (*Mahāparinirvāṇa*). Both follow the orthodox traditions,[1] but the workmanship is of the poorest kind. Obviously it is late and decadent, but it is the sort of relief that an incompetent craftsman might have turned out at any time after about A.D. 200. On the other hand, the decadence of fig. 151 is due less to the personal shortcomings of the sculptor than to the general decline of the period. We shall appreciate this if we compare fig. 151 with the other reliefs of the same scene—the Grand Miracle of Śrāvastī—illustrated in figs. 122–5. Even the latest and most decadent of these, fig. 123, is substantially less degenerate in style than fig. 151; and this is true not only of the general design, which in fig. 151 is almost geometric in its formality, but of the individual figures which are copies of conventional types without any trace of creative imagination.

[1] For earlier examples of the Death Scene, see figs. 68, 72, 87, 127, 128 and 129.

## CHAPTER 12

# CONCLUSION

(FIG. 152)

Such, in rough outline, is the story of the Early School of Buddhist art in Gandhāra, as revealed by my discoveries at Taxila. Now that we know the truth and can follow, step by step, the course of its evolution, we may wonder why earlier efforts at its reconstruction fell so wide of the mark. Still more may we wonder at the way in which even the highest authorities on the subject failed to distinguish between this Early School of Gandhāra art and the Later School which was flourishing between the latter part of the fourth century and towards the end of the fifth century of our era. For, although these two Schools had a common ancestry (although, indeed, one sprang phoenix-like from the ashes of the other), the differences between them are so glaring that they might well have been recognized long before Taxila yielded its clear and conclusive evidence. Let us consider what these differences were.

In the Early School the sculptors worked almost exclusively in stone suitable for fine carving. Doubtless they were familiar with clay and terracotta, but, so far as I am aware, not a single figure in any of these materials which is referable to this Early School has survived throughout the length and breadth of Gandhāra; and even at Taxila, where no suitable stone was available, there is only one example of relief work in lime-stucco dating from this period. In the Later School, on the other hand, sculptors worked all but exclusively in lime-stucco or clay, sometimes burnt into terracotta, clay being commonly in positions protected from the weather, lime-stucco and terracotta in more exposed ones. No doubt the adoption of these materials in place of the earlier stone was due primarily to the demand for sculpture in districts where there was no stone suitable for fine carving, but where there was no shortage of limestone or clay. This was eminently the case at Taxila, the largest city in the North-West and the oldest and greatest stronghold of Buddhism, where the only two local stones are a flint-like limestone, of which the hills are composed, and a coarse sandstone, which could be employed for images such as those illustrated in figs. 27 and 28, but did not lend itself to finer work.

And this brings us to the second outstanding difference between the two Schools, namely, the extent of the areas in which they flourished. Whereas the Earlier School was limited to the Peshāwar Valley and neighbouring tracts west of the Indus, where the indispensable schist and other fine-grained stones could be quarried, the Later School extended over a much wider area, from Taxila east of the Indus as far to the north-west as ancient Bactria and the banks of the Oxus. It was because of the wide extent of this School in Pakistan, India and Afghānistān, far beyond the boundaries of Gandhāra, that in my book *Taxila* I adopted for it the designation of 'Indo-Afghan'. This I did after consulting with the Director of the French Mission in Afghānistān, M. J. Hackin, and I still incline to believe that in many ways that designation was preferable to 'Later Gandhāra School', which, in deference to some of my critics, I have substituted in the present publication. For, notwithstanding the admittedly close relationship between the two Schools, it is manifestly desirable to employ a term which will avoid any risk of confusing one School with the other and at the same time to give some idea of the different areas in which the two Schools flourished, and to indicate that the second School was in all probability developed on the soil of Afghānistān, not in Gandhāra.

Thirdly, apart from the materials of which they were made, there were signal differences in the essential character of the sculptures of the two Schools as well as in the design of the structures on which they were displayed. At the time when the Early School first took shape, the stūpa was still the dominant object of cult worship, as it had been in the Early Indian School, and in all important *saṅghārāmas* there was a large central stūpa encompassed by a number of relatively small votive stūpas. It was on the adornment of these latter monuments that the stone reliefs described in this book were for the most part employed, a few only serving as ex-voto offerings which were subsequently collected and housed in buildings set apart for the purpose, and a few also for the enrichment of minor architectural members such as the risers in the great stairway at Jamāl-Garhī. At the period of which we are speaking the small votive stūpa generally took a simple form, consisting of a square or circular base with a cylindrical drum and dome above, and one or more umbrellas crowning the whole; but with the passing years many small modifications were introduced into this simple design, and variety was imparted to it by the diverse character of the pictorial reliefs and decorative carvings which embellished the surface of the monument.

As in the Early Indian School, the subjects of these reliefs were the Birth (*Jātaka*) stories of the Buddha in his previous lives and the chief events in his last life, but in Gandhāran art the former are much rarer than they had been in the older art of India. By the time the Later Gandhāra School emerged, the form and decoration of stūpas, both large and small, had undergone radical changes. Their bases were now split up into two or more receding terraces, and these in turn were covered with lines of Buddha or Bodhisattva figures set in ornamental niches and divided one from another by stunted pilasters of debased Corinthian pattern. For by this time the Buddha or Bodhisattva images had become supreme and ubiquitous as objects of adoration, and were being endlessly multiplied on every imaginable scale, from the tiny figures impressed on clay sealings and buried in the heart of stūpas to the colossal cult statues enshrined in chapels, 30 ft. and more in height. And this kind of decoration, with its myriads of duplicated figures, was, of course, at once facilitated and encouraged by the use of clay and stucco in place of stone, since it was now possible to cast the images and architectural embellishments in moulds, and to repeat them indefinitely and with the least possible labour over the surface of a monument.

But, though the new clay or stucco technique was productive of a vast amount of indifferent, careless and unimaginative work, it also lent itself, in the hands of the more gifted artists, to work of a higher order than anything of which the Earlier School had shown itself capable—work which was remarkable for its command of form and vitality of expression, coupled in some cases with a spirituality which anticipated the best efforts of the Gupta Age in India. Here I can give no more than a single example of the striking differences which in this respect distinguish the sculpture of the Earlier and Later Schools. It concerns the Bodhisattva images. Among the finest known specimens of such images belonging to the Earlier School are those illustrated in figs. 137 and 138. The outstanding characteristics of these two figures are, on the one hand, their superb execution with its clean, clear-cut chiselling and elaborate decoration; on the other, their air of foppishness and swagger, eminently suited to a royal prince, but less so to a Bodhisattva, whatever his royal parentage. Of any expression of spirituality in these statues there is not a trace. But now turn to the last illustration in this book—a Bodhisattva head of the Later School from a group at the Kālawān Monastery at Taxila, and mark the look of dignified composure, peace and compassion. In the whole realm of Buddhist art there is surely no image of a Bodhisattva in which the artist has succeeded so well in 'incarnating spirit in matter'.

I hope that I have now said enough to give the reader some idea of the radical differences which distinguish the Earlier and Later Schools of Gandhāran art. Such differences imply a long and active period of evolution between the eclipse of the Earlier School in the first half of the third century A.D. and the appearance of the Later School in the second half of the fourth century. What happened during this century and a half? No connecting links between the two Schools have yet been found in the Panjāb or North-West Frontier; nor, for two very good reasons, does there seem any likelihood of their being found on the soil of Pakistan. The first reason is that the whole of that terrain has already been relatively well explored and it is hardly believable that the existence of such remains, which must have been both widespread and abundant, could have escaped all observation. The second reason is that the Early Gandhāra School owed its development mainly to the patronage which the imperial Kushān rulers, from Kadphises I to Vāsudeva, gave to Buddhism, and the eclipse of the School came, suddenly and completely, when the Kushān power was broken, the Buddhist monasteries destroyed and the Kushāns themselves driven back to their former home in Bactria. It was there, in the north of the modern Afghānistān, where the Kushāns had long before become imbued with the brilliant cultural legacy of provincial Hellenism, that we must, in my view, look for the missing links between the Early School of Gandhāra and that Later and very different School of Art which the Kushāns brought back with them when they returned to the North-West in the second half of the fourth century, and which was flourishing there so richly and luxuriantly until the final overthrow of the Kushāns and the utter destruction of the Buddhist monasteries at the hands of the White Huns.

# INDEX

*The entries refer only to items of art-historical and iconographical interest*

**Fig. 1.** Symbol of the Three Jewels (*triratna*)—the Buddha, the Law and the Order— attended by a guardian *yaksha*. On the summit of the Northern Gateway of the Great Stūpa at Sāñchī. Marshall and Foucher, *Monuments of Sāñchī*, vol. II, pl. 30.

Fig. 2. *Yaksha* sprites (*kumbhaṇḍas*) spouting forth the lotus—emblem in ancient India of Birth and Life and Good Fortune. On the Southern Gateway of the Great Stūpa at Sāñchī. Marshall and Foucher, *Monuments of Sāñchī*, vol. I, p. 146; vol. II, pl. 11.

Fig. 3. Queen Māyā on lotus, symbol of the divine Birth of the Buddha. On the Eastern Gateway of the Great Stūpa at Sāñchī. Marshall and Foucher, *Monuments of Sāñchī*, vol. I, pp. 183 and 197; vol. II, pl. 41

(*b*)

(*a*)

Fig. 4 (*a*). Bodhi-tree and throne, symbolizing the Illumination. (*b*) Wheel of the Law, symbolizing the First Sermon. On the Gateway of Stūpa 3 at Sāñchī. *Ibid.* vol. III, pl. 103*e*.

Fig. 5. Adoration of a stūpa, symbolizing the Death of the Buddha. On the Western Gateway of the Great Stūpa at Sāñchī. *Ibid.* vol. II, pl. 63.

Fig. 6. The latter part of the Viśvantara Jātaka. On the Northern Gateway of the Great Stūpa at Sāñchī. Marshall and Foucher, *Monuments of Sāñchī*, vol. II, pl. 29.

# PLATE 5

**Fig. 7.** Assault and defeat of Māra. On the Western Gateway of the Great Stūpa at Sāñchī. Marshall and Foucher, *Monuments of Sāñchī,* vol. I, pp. 114–15; vol. II, pl. 61.

**Fig. 8.** Procession of King Śuddhodana to meet his son on his return to Kapilavastu. On the Eastern Gateway of the Great Stūpa at Sāñchī. Marshall and Foucher, *Monuments of Sāñchī*, vol. I, pp. 122–3; vol. II, pl. 50.

**Fig. 9.** Three of the six inferior heavens (*kāmāvacara*). On the Eastern Gateway of the Great Stūpa at Sāñchī. Marshall and Foucher, *Monuments of Sāñchī*, vol. I, p. 227; vol. II, pl. 49*a*.

(*a*)

(*b*)

**Fig. 10.** (*a*) The Śyāma Jātaka. On the Western Gateway of the Great Stūpa at Sāñchī. Marshall and Foucher, *Monuments of Sāñchī*, vol. I, p. 225; vol. II, pl. 65*a* 1. (*b*) The Nāga-rāja Mucilinda. On the Western Gateway of the Great Stūpa at Sāñchī. *Ibid.* vol. I, p. 208; vol. II, pl. 65*a* 2.

**Fig. 11.** A scene of pleasure among the rocks. On the Northern Gateway of the Great Stūpa at Sāñchī. Marshall and Foucher, *Monuments of Sāñchī*, vol. I, pp. 228–9; vol. II, pl. 34*b* 2.

**Fig. 12.** Dwarf Atlants (*kumbhaṇḍas*). On the Western Gateway of the Great Stūpa at Sāñchī. Marshall and Foucher, *Monuments of Sāñchī*, vol. I, pp. 14c–1; vol. II, pl. 57.

**Fig. 13.** Toilet-tray with pair of lovers. From Sirkap. National Museum of Pakistan, Karachi. Diam. 4.31 in. Grey schist. Marshall, *Taxila*, vol. II, p. 494, no. 62; vol. III, pl. 144, no. 62.

**Fig. 14.** Toilet-tray with drinking-scene. From Sirkap. National Museum of Pakistan, Karachi. Diam. 5.31 in. Grey schist. Marshall, *Taxila*, vol. II, pp. 494–5, no. 63; vol. III, pl, 144, no. 63.

**Fig. 15.** Toilet-tray with hippocamp and rider. From Sirkap. Taxila Museum. Diam. 4.62 in. Grey schist. Marshall, *Taxila*, vol. II, p. 496, no. 74; vol. III, pl. 144, no. 74.

**Fig. 16.** Toilet-tray with crowded drinking-scene. From Sirkap. National Museum, New Delhi. Diam. 6.2 in. Greenish-grey steatite. Marshall, *Taxila*, vol. II, p. 495, no. 65; vol. III, pl. 144, no. 65.

Fig. 17. Toilet-tray with sea-monster, ridden by half-draped female with baby. From Sirkap. Taxila Museum. Diam. 3.12 in. Steatite. Marshall, *Taxila*, vol. II, p. 496, no. 76; vol. III, pl. 145, no. 76.

Fig. 18. Toilet-tray with Aphrodite and winged Erotes. From Narai, Peshāwar District. Formerly in L. W. Jardine Collection. Diam. 4.75 in.

# PLATE 17

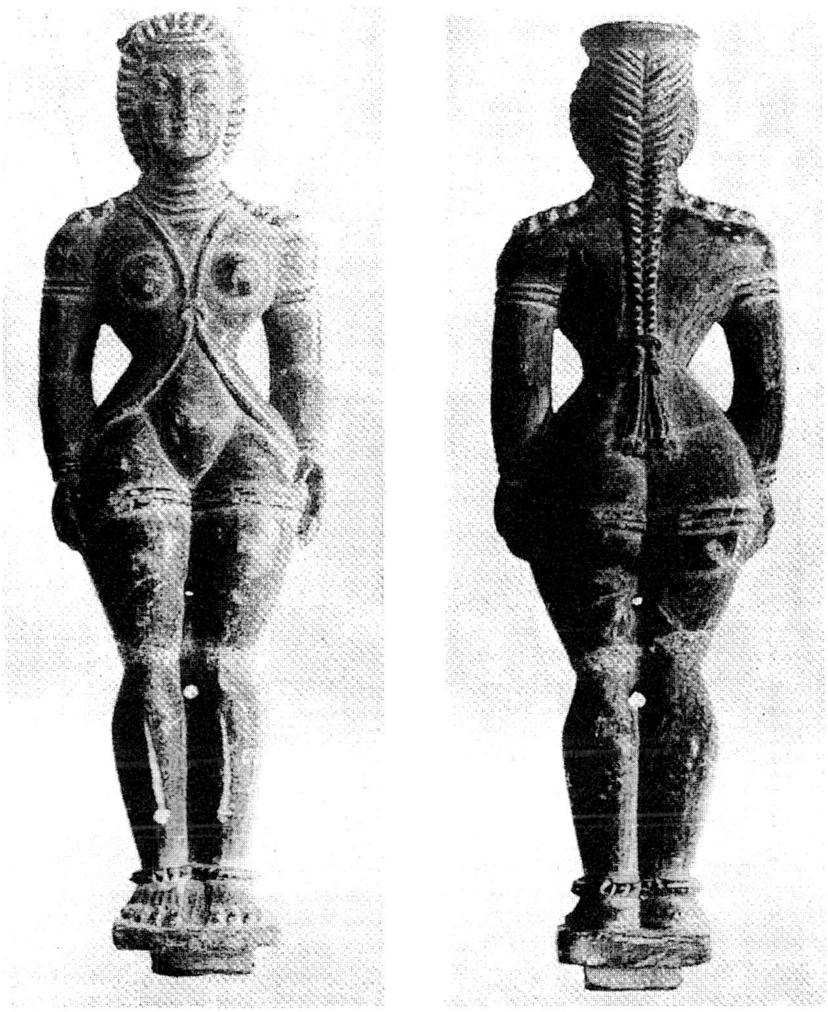

(*a*) (*b*)

**Fig. 19.** Female statuette. From Sirkap. National Museum of Pakistan, Karachi. Ht. 7.25 in. Chloritic micaceous schist. Marshall, *Taxila*, vol. II, p. 701, no. 4; vol. III, pl. 211, no. 4*a* and *b*.

Fig. 20. Female statuette. From Block D', Sirkap. National Museum of Pakistan, Karachi. Ht. 9 in. Chloritic micaceous schist. Marshall, *Taxila*, vol. II, p. 701, no. 3; vol. III, pl. 211, no. 3*a* and *b*.

**Fig. 21.** Bracket in form of a winged *deva*. From Sirkap. Taxila Museum. Ht. 4.75 in. Chloritized micaceous schist. Marshall, *Taxila*, vol. II, p. 702, no. 8; vol. III, pl. 212, no. 8.

**Fig. 22.** Inscribed bracket in form of a winged *deva*. From Sirkap. Taxila Museum. Length 6.62 in. Pale chloritized micaceous schist. *Ibid.* vol. II, p. 702, no. 11; vol. III, pl. 213, no. 11.

Fig. 23. Bracket in form of a winged *deva*. From Kunāla. Taxila Museum. Length 7.5 in. Micaceous schist. Marshall, *Taxila*, vol. II, p. 703, no. 18; vol. III, pl. 213, no. 18.

Fig. 24. Bracket in form of a winged *deva*. From Dharmarājikā(?). British Museum. Ht. 15.75 in. Talcose schist. *A.G.-B.G.* vol. I, p. 213, fig. 89.

Fig. 25. Bracket in form of a winged *devī*. From Dharmarājikā. Taxila Museum. Length 13.5 in. Quartz schist. Marshall, *Taxila*, vol. II, p. 703, no. 16; vol. III, pl. 213, no. 16.

Fig. 26. Unidentified Jātaka. From Block E, Sirkap. Taxila Museum. Ht. 13.25 in. Micaceous schist. Marshall, *Taxila*, vol. II, p. 721, no. 135; vol. III, pl. 222, no. 135.

**Fig. 27.** Male statuette, possibly representing Sūrya, the sun-god. From Sirkap. Taxila Museum. Ht. 26.25 in. Tarakī sandstone. Marshall, *Taxila*, vol. II, p. 702, no. 7; vol. III, pl. 212, no. 7.

**Fig. 28.** Image of Gautama. From Dharmarājikā. Taxila Museum. Ht. 16 in. Tarakī sandstone. *Ibid.* vol. II, p. 701, no. 6; vol. III, pl. 212, no. 6.

**Fig. 29.** Head of Dionysus. From Sirkap. National Museum of Pakistan, Karachi. Ht. 3.75 in. Silver repoussé. Marshall, *Taxila*, vol. II, p. 614, no. 21; vol. III, pl. 209*a*.

**Fig. 30.** Statuette of Egyptian child-god Harpocrates. From Sirkap. National Museum of Pakistan, Karachi. Ht. 5 in. Bronze. *Ibid.* II, p. 605, no. 417; III, pl. 186*e*.

**Fig. 31.** Female head. From Sirkap. National Museum of Pakistan, Karachi. Ht. 2.37 in. Buff-coloured terra-cotta. *Ibid.* vol. II, p. 451, no. 47; vol. III, pl. 133, no. 47.

Fig. 32. Head of Satyr. Ht. 8.12 in.

Fig. 34. Ht. 6 in.

Fig. 33. Ht. 4.5 in.

Fig. 35. Ht. 3.75 in.

Stucco heads from Apsidal Temple in Sirkap. 32: National Museum of Pakistan, Karachi; 33–5: Taxila Museum. Cf. Marshall, *Taxila*, vol. II, pp. 517–19, nos. 1, 2, 3, 10; vol. III, pl. 148, nos. 1, 2, 3, 10.

Fig. 36. Ht. 4.5 in.

Fig. 38. Head of Bodhisattva. Ht. 4.75 in.

Fig. 37. Ht. 6.5 in.

Fig. 39. Head of colossal Bodhisattva. Ht. 13.5 in.

Stucco heads from Apsidal Temple in Sirkap. 36: National Museum, New Delhi; 37–9: Taxila Museum. Marshall, *Taxila*, vol. II, pp. 518–19, nos. 8, 11, 20, 19; vol. III, pl. 148, nos. 8, 11: pl. 149*c, h*.

**Fig. 40.** Drinking-party of nine figures. Probably from Swāt. Guides' Mess, Mardān; now in Peshāwar Museum. Ht. 4.75 in. *A.G-B.G.* vol. 1, p. 253, fig. 131.

**Fig. 41.** So-called 'Presentation of the Bride to Siddhārtha'. From Takht-i-Bahī. Ht. 5.5 in. British Museum.

Fig. 43. Ht. 6.9 in.

Fig. 42. Silver Parthian goblet. From Sirkap. Taxila Museum. Ht. 5.25 in. Marshall, *Taxila*, vol. II, p. 612, 5*a*; vol. III, pl. 188, 5*a*.

Fig. 44. Ht. 6.75 in.

Figs. 43, 44. Reliefs formerly in the Church Missionary Society's Collection, Peshāwar; now in Peshāwar Museum.

Fig. 45.

Fig. 46.

Figs. 45, 46. Reliefs formerly in the possession of the Church Missionary Society at Peshāwar. Fig. 46 is now in the Peshāwar Museum.

**Fig. 47.** Sea or river deities. British Museum. Ht. 6.75 in. *A.G-B.G.* Vol. I, p. 247, fig. 126.

**Fig. 48.** Triton in triangular panel. British Museum. Ht. 7.5 in. *A.G-B.G.* vol. I, p. 243, fig. 123.

**Fig. 49.** Family drinking-scene of five figures. From Haḍḍa, S. Afghānistān Musée Guimet, Paris. Ht. 6.5 in.

**Fig. 50.** Family drinking-scene. From Haḍḍa, S. Afghānistān. Kābul Museum. Ht. 6.5 in.

**Fig. 51.** Drinking-scene of two couples, carved on lion-footed pedestal. Lahore Museum. Ht. 9.25 in. *A.G.-B.G.* vol. I, p. 251, fig. 130.

**Fig. 52.** Crouching Atlant. Lahore Museum.

Fig. 53. Gift of the Jetavana Garden. Guides' Mess, Mardān; now in Peshāwar Museum. Ht. 8 in. *A.G.-B.G.* vol. I, p. 474, fig. 239.

**Fig. 54.** The Interpretation of Māyā's dream. From Swāt. Guides' Mess, Mardān; now in Peshāwar Museum. Ht. 6 in. *A.G.-B.G.* vol. I, p. 299, fig. 151. Photograph by Mr Caddy.

**Fig. 55.** The Seven Steps of the Infant Buddha. From Swāt. Guides' Mess, Mardān; now in Peshāwar Museum. Ht. 6 in. *A.G.-B.G.* vol. I, p. 307, fig. 155. Photograph by Mr Caddy.

**Fig. 56.** Duplicate of Fig. 54. Photograph by Archaeological Department.

**Fig. 57.** Duplicate of Fig. 55. Photograph by Archaeological Department.

**Fig. 58.** Bath of the Infant Buddha. From Swāt. Guides' Mess, Mardān; now in Peshāwar Museum. Ht. 10.5 in. *A.G.-B.G.* vol. I, p. 309, fig. 156.

Fig. 60. *Deva*. From Dharmarājikā at Taxila. Taxila Museum. Ht. 13.5 in. Chloritized micaceous schist.

Fig. 59. The First Sermon. From Loriyān Tangai. Calcutta Museum. Ht. 12.6 in. *A.G.-B.G.* vol. 1, p. 431, fig. 219.

**Fig. 61.** The gift of the bundle of grass. Guides' Mess, Mardān; now in Peshāwar Museum. Ht. 15.6 in.

Fig. 62. Adoration of the Bodhisattva's head-dress in the Trayastrimśa Heaven. Guides' Mess, Mardān; now in Peshāwar Museum. Ht. 15.1 in.

Fig. 63. The Buddha and Vajrapāṇi. Berlin Museum. Ht. 15.75 in.
*A.G.-B.G.* vol. II, part I, p. 49, fig. 326.

Fig. 64. Female guard, with shield and spear. Guides' Mess, Mardān; now in Peshāwar Museum. Ht. 15 in.

Fig. 65. Musician playing on lute. From Swāt. Guides' Mess, Mardān; now in Peshāwar Museum. Ht. 15.1 in.

**Fig. 66.** The Buddha and a Brāhman ascetic. Guides' Mess, Mardān; now in Peshāwar Museum. Ht. 15 in.

Fig. 67. The attack of Māra. Guides' Mess, Mardān; now in Peshāwar Museum. Ht. 15.25 in.

Fig. 68. *Mahāparinirvāṇa* of the Buddha. Guides' Mess, Mardān; now in Peshāwar Museum. Ht. 10.5 in. *A.G.-B.G.* vol. I, p. 557, fig. 276.

**Fig. 69.** Submission of the Nāga Apalāla. From Sanghao. Bombay Museum. Ht. 7.12 in.
*A.G.-B.G.* vol. I, p. 551, fig. 274.

Fig. 70. The Worship of the Three Jewels. From Lower Monastery at Nathu. Calcutta Museum. Ht. 8.75 in. *A.G.-B.G.* vol. I, p. 428, fig. 216.

**Fig. 71.** Gautama and the Brāhman ascetics. From Rhode, near Sanghao. Lahore Museum. Ht. 6.3 in. *A.G.-B.G.* vol. I, p. 377, fig. 191.

Fig. 72. *Mahāparinirvāṇa* of the Buddha. From Lower Monastery at Nathu. Lahore Museum. Ht. 9.12 in. *A.G.-B.G.* vol. I, p. 565, fig. 281.

Fig. 73. Dipaṅkara Jātaka. From Sikri. Lahore Museum. Ht. 13 in.

Fig. 74. The Bodhisattva in the Tushita heaven. From Sikri. Lahore Museum. Ht. 13 in.

Fig. 75. The Buddha and the Nāga-rāja Kālika. From Sikri. Lahore Museum. Ht. 13 in.

Fig. 76. The Buddha and the grass-cutter Svastika. From Sikri. Lahore Museum. Ht. 13 in. *A.G.-B.G.* vol. I, p. 391, fig. 197.

Fig. 77. Presentation of the four begging-bowls. From Sikri. Lahore Museum. Ht. 13 in.

PLATE 54

Fig. 78. *Yaksha* with grape-vine scroll. Provenance not known. Peshāwar Museum.

Fig. 79. Door-jamb with empanelled figures. From Dharmarājikā Stūpa. Taxila Museum. Ht. 26.5 in. Chloritized micaceous schist.

**Fig. 80.** Fragment of a frieze with busts of celestials beneath arches. From Dharmarājikā Stūpa. Taxila Museum. Length 6.5 in. Chloritized micaceous schist. Marshall, *Taxila*, vol. II, p. 710, no. 78; vol. III, pl. 217, no. 78.

**Fig. 81.** Fragment of a frieze, decorated with intertwined vine stems. From Dharmarājikā. Taxila Museum. Length 7.25 in. Chloritic micaceous schist. *Ibid.* vol. II, p. 710, no. 81.

**Fig. 82.** Nāga-rāja with musicians and attendants. From Kāfir-kot. British Museum. Length 22.75 in. *A.G.-B.G.* vol. I, p. 253, fig. 133*b*, and p. 256.

**Fig. 83.** Drinking-scene of Nāga-rāja and queen. From Kāfir-kot. British Museum. Length 24.25 in. *Ibid.* vol. I, p. 253, fig. 133*a*, and p. 256.

**Fig. 84.** The starving Bodhisattva. Probably from Jamāl-Garhī. British Museum. Ht. 7 in. *A.G.-B.G.* vol. 1, p. 381, fig. 193.

Fig. 85. Cult statue of the Buddha. Lahore Museum.

**Fig. 86.** Cult statue of the Buddha. Lahore Museum. Ht. 4 ft. 5 in.

Fig. 87. *Mahāparinirvāṇa* of the Buddha. From Upper Monastery at Nathu. Calcutta Museum. Ht. 8.75 in.

Fig. 88. Presentation to the Buddha of a mango grove by the courtesan Āmrapālī. From Upper Monastery at Nathu. Calcutta Museum.

**Fig. 89.** *Yakshī* standing beneath a *śāla* tree. From Upper Monastery at Nathu. Calcutta Museum. Ht. 13.5 in.

**Fig. 90.** Fragment showing portions of five figures. From Loriyān Tangai. Calcutta Museum. Ht. 11 in.

**Fig. 91.** Base ornamented with garland and Erotes. From Lower Monastery at Nathu. Calcutta Museum. Ht. 7.5 in.

**Fig. 92.** Sleep of the women. From Takht-i-Bahī. British Museum. Ht. 6 in.
*A.G.-B.G.* vol. I, p. 351, fig. 179.

**Fig. 93.** Fragment from a scene of the Sleeping Women. From Dharmarājikā. Taxila Museum. Ht. 19.5 in. Phyllite. Marshall, *Taxila*, vol. II, pp. 713–14, no. 99; vol. III, pl. 218, no. 99.

**Fig. 94.** Māyā's dream. From Kālawān Monastery. National Museum, New Delhi. Length 15.6 in. Phyllite. Marshall, *Taxila*, vol. II, p. 712, no. 92; vol. III, pl. 218, no. 92.

**Fig. 95.** The child Bodhisattva going to school in a ram-cart. From Chārsada Tehsīl, Peshāwar District. Victoria and Albert Museum, London. Ht. 14 in.

**Fig. 96.** The Buddha in unidentified scene. From Palātu-Dheṛī, Chārsada. Peshāwar Museum. Ht. 14 in. *A.S.R.* 1902–3, p. 169, no. 28 and pl. XXVII, 5.

Fig. 97. Adoration of a stūpa. From Swāt. British Museum. Ht. 6 in.

**Fig. 98.** The Buddha enthroned with Vajrapāṇi and seven female devotees. From Dharmarājikā. Taxila Museum. Ht. 19 in. Phyllite. Marshall, *Taxila*, vol. II, p. 718, no. 121; vol. III, pl. 221, no. 121.

**Fig. 99.** Birth of the Buddha. Provenance unknown. Peshāwar Museum.

**Fig. 100.** Miracle at Śrāvastī. From Dharmarājikā. Taxila Museum. Ht. 11 in. Phyllite. Marshall, *Taxila*, vol. II, p. 720, no. 132; vol. III, pl. 222, no. 132.

# PLATE 71

**Fig. 101.** The Buddha under pipal canopy. From Dharmarājikā. Taxila Museum. Ht. 9.5 in Phyllite. Marshall, *Taxila*, vol. II, pp. 721–2, no. 141; vol. III, pl. 224, no. 141.

**Fig. 102.** Entreaty of the gods in the Tushita heaven. From Dharmarājikā. Taxila Museum. Ht. 8.75 in. Phyllite. Marshall, *Taxila*, vol. II, p. 712, no. 93; vol. III, pl. 217, no. 93.

(*b*)

(*a*)

Fig. 103. Part of a stele. (*a*) Submission of Nāga Apalāla. (*b*) Unidentified. From Jamāl-Garhī. Calcutta Museum. Ht. 22.8 in. *A.G.-B.G.* vol. I, p. 549, fig. 272.

Fig. 104. Birth of Chandaka and Kaṇṭhaka. From Jamāl-Garhī. Calcutta Museum. Ht. 9 in. *A.G.-B.G.* vol. I, p. 318, fig. 163.

Fig. 105. Wrestling match. From Jamāl-Garhī. Calcutta Museum. Ht. 11 in. *Ibid.* vol. II, p. 11, fig. 303.

(*b*) ←

→ (*a*)

**Fig. 106.** Śyāma Jātaka. From Dharmarājikā. Taxila Museum. Length 2 ft. 11 in. Phyllite. Marshall, *Taxila*, vol. II, pp. 711–12, nos. 90*a* and *b*; vol. III, pl. 217, nos. 90*a* and *b*.

Fig. 107. Visit of Indra to the Buddha. From Giri, Taxila. Taxila Museum. Ht. 21.25 in. Phyllite. Marshall, *Taxila*, vol. II, p. 716, no. 113; vol. III, pl. 219, no. 113.

**Fig. 108.** A *yaksha* Atlant. From Jamāl-Garhī. Calcutta Museum. Ht. 7.5 in. *A.G.-B.G.* vol. I, p. 209, fig. 87.

**Fig. 109.** Head of the Buddha. From Mohṛā Morādu. Taxila Museum. Ht. 5 in. Talcose chloritic schist. Marshall, *Taxila*, vol. II, p. 724, no. 159.

Fig. 110. The Buddha. Lahore Museum. Ht. 3 ft. 5 in.

# PLATE 77

**Fig. 111.** The Buddha. From Dharmarājikā. Taxila Museum. Ht. 3 ft. 1 in. Phyllite. Marshall, *Taxila*, vol. II, p. 724, no. 158; vol. III, pl. 225, no. 158.

**Fig. 112.** Hāritī. From Taxila-i-Bahī. Peshāwar Museum. *A.G.-B.G.* vol. II, p. 129, fig. 376.

Fig. 113. Miracle of the black snake at Rājagṛiha. From Rāṇīgat(?). Lahore Museum. Ht. 13.5 in. *A.G.-B.G.* vol. I, p. 453, fig. 227.

**Fig. 114.** The Buddha's Flight from the City and connected scenes. Lahore Museum. Ht. 24.5 in.

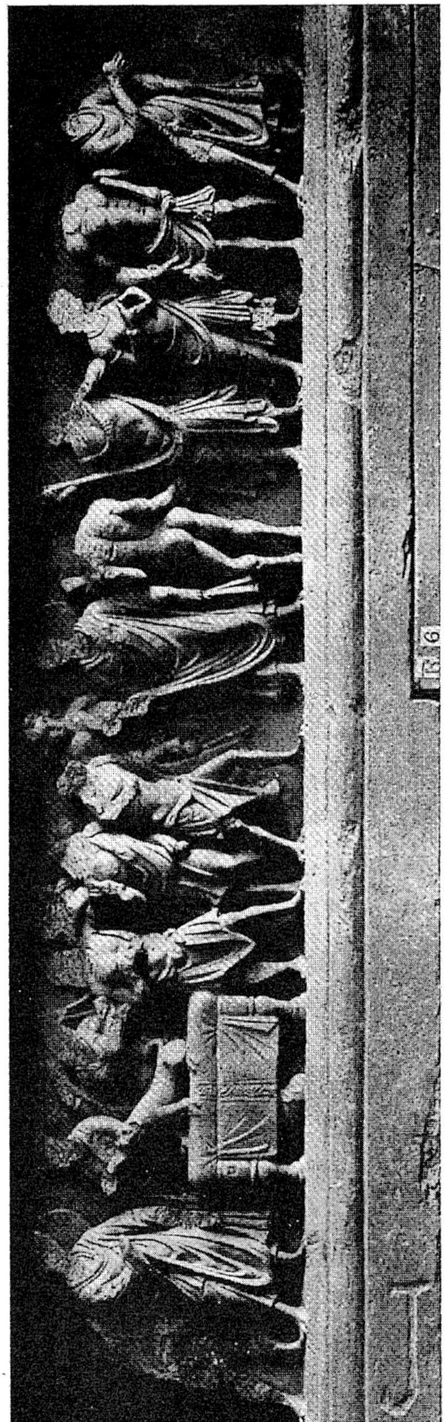

Fig. 115. Miracles at Śrāvastī and Uruvilvā. From Jamāl-Garhī. Calcutta Museum. Ht. 7·5 in.

**Fig. 116.** Three scenes from the story of Nanda. From Jamāl-Garhī. Calcutta Museum. Ht. 23.75 in. *A.G.-B.G.* vol. I, p. 471, fig. 238.

**Fig. 117.** The First Sermon. From Loriyān Tangai. Calcutta Museum. Ht. 15.5 in. *A.G.-B.G.* vol. 1, p. 433, fig. 220.

Fig. 118. Visit of Indra to the Buddha. From Loriyān Tangai. Calcutta Museum.
Ht. 3 ft. 9 in. *A.G.-B.G.* vol. I, p. 493, fig. 246.

# PLATE 84

**Fig. 119.** Flight of the Bodhisattva from Kapilavastu. From Loriyān Tangai. Calcutta Museum. Ht. 1 ft. 7 in. *A.G.-B.G.* vol. I, p. 357, fig. 182.

**Fig. 120.** Visit of Indra to the Buddha. From Mamāne-Dheṛī, near Chārsada. Peshāwar Museum. Ht. 30 in. *C.I.I.* vol. II, p. 171 and pl. XXXIV.

**Fig. 121.** Conversion of Nanda. The enticement scene. From Haḍḍa, S. Afghānistān. British Museum. Ht. 11.75 in. Limestone. *A.G.-B.G.* vol. I, p. 465, fig. 234.

**Fig. 122.** Miracle of Śrāvastī. From Loriyān Tangai. Calcutta Museum. Ht. 39.5 in. *A.G.-B.G.* vol. 1, p. 192, fig. 76.

**Fig. 123.** Miracle of Śrāvastī. From Muhammad Nāri. Lahore Museum. Ht. 3 ft. 5 in. *A.G.-B.G.* vol. I, p. 193, fig. 77.

**Fig. 124.** Miracle of Śrāvastī. From Sahrī-Bahlol. Peshāwar Museum. Ht. 21.5 in. Hargreaves, *Handbook to the Sculptures in the Peshāwar Museum*, p. 42, pl. 2.

**Fig. 125.** Miracle of Śrāvastī. From Sahrī-Bahlol. Peshāwar Museum.

**Fig. 126.** Ornamental canopy. From Sahrī-Bahlol. Peshāwar Museum.

**Fig. 127.** The death of the Buddha (*mahāparinirvāṇa*). From Swāt. Calcutta Museum. Ht. 10 in. *A.G.-B.G.* vol. 1, p. 561, fig. 279.

Fig. 128. The death of the Buddha (*mahāparinirvāṇa*). From Swāt. Calcutta Museum. Ht. 16.25 in. *A.G.-B.G.* vol. 1, p. 558, Fig. 277.

**Fig. 129.** The death of the Buddha (*mahāparinirvāṇa*). From Takht-i-Bahī. British Museum. Ht. 10.5 in. *A.G.-B.G.* vol. I, p. 559, fig. 278.

**Fig. 130.** Viśvantara Jātaka. British Museum. Ht. 9.25 in.

PLATE 94

**Fig. 131.** The Buddha, standing in *abhaya-mudrā*.
Lahore Museum (no. 740).

**Fig. 132.** Standing image of the Buddha. Formerly in Guides' Mess, Mardān. Ht. of head, 10.8 in. *A.G.-B.G.* vol. II, p. 291, fig. 445. Foucher, *Beginnings of Buddhist Art*, p. 119 and pl. XI, 2.

**Fig. 133.** The Buddha and the Kāśyapas. From Sahrī-Bahlol. Peshāwar Museum. Ht. 20.5 in. *A.G.-B.G.* vol. II, p. 343, fig. 461.

Fig. 134. Standing image of the Buddha. From Mamāne-Dheṛī. Peshāwar Museum. Ht. 3 ft. 1 in.

**Fig. 135.** Seated image of the Buddha in *dhyāna-mudrā*.
From Takht-i-Bahī. Peshāwar Museum.

**Fig. 136.** Seated image of the Buddha in *dhyāna-mudrā*.
From Sahrī-Bahlol. Peshāwar Museum. Ht. 2 ft. 5.5 in.

**Fig. 137.** Bodhisattva Maitreya. From Mohṛā Morādu monastery, Taxila. Taxila Museum. Ht. 3 ft. 4 in. Phyllite. Marshall, *Taxila*, vol. II, p. 722, no. 142; vol. III, pl. 223.

Fig. 138. Bust of Bodhisattva. Guides' Mess, Mardān; now in Peshāwar Museum.

**Fig. 139.** Standing image of Bodhisattva Maitreya. From Sahrī-Bahlol. Peshāwar Museum. Ht. 3 ft. 2 in. *A.G.-B.G.* vol. II, p. 221, fig. 416.

**Fig. 140.** Bodhisattva Maitreya. Lahore Museum. Ht. 2 ft. 9 in.

**Fig. 141.** Bodhisattva Siddhārtha meditating at the Ploughing Festival. From Sahrī-Bahlol. Peshāwar Museum. Ht. 28 in. *A.G.-B.G.* vol. II, p. 217, fig. 413.

**Fig. 142.** Bodhisattva Maitreya. From Upper Monastery at Nathu. Calcutta Museum. Ht. 14 in. *A.M.I.* pl. 93.

**Fig. 143.** Seated image of Pāñcika. From Tahkal, near Peshāwar. Lahore Museum. Ht. 5 ft. 11 in. *A.G.-B.G.* vol. II, pp. 108–9, figs. 367–8.

**Fig. 144.** Pāñcika and Hārītī. From Sahrī-Bahlol. Peshāwar Museum. Ht. 3 ft. 4 in. Hargreaves, *Handbook to Sculptures in Peshāwar Museum*, pp. 44 and 50, pl. 7.

Fig. 145. Atlant. From Kāli Ghund, Mardān District. Peshāwar Museum. Ht. 21.75 in.

Fig. 146. Atlant. From Jamāl-Garhī. Calcutta Museum. Ht. 7.5 in.

**Fig. 147.** Corinthian capital. From Jamāl-Garhī. Calcutta Museum. Length 2 ft. 10 in. *A.G.-B.G.* vol. I, p. 235, fig. 112, and *A.M.I.* pl. 77.

**Fig. 148.** Frieze of garland and amorini. From Kālawān, Taxila. National Museum of Pakistan, Karachi. Length 15 in. Phyllite. Marshall, *Taxila*, vol. II, p. 709, no. 72; vol. III, pl. 216, no. 72.

**Fig. 149.** Door-jamb. From Dharmarājikā. Taxila Museum. Ht. 22.75 in. Phyllite. Marshall, *Taxila*, vol. II, p. 704, no. 22; vol. III, pl, 214, no. 22.

**Fig. 150.** Panel with two scenes, (*a*) presentation of the four bowls, (*b*) death of the Buddha. From Afrido-Dheṛī(?). Peshāwar Museum.

Fig. 151. The Grand Miracle of Śrāvastī. Peshāwar Museum.

**Fig. 152.** Terracotta head of Bodhisattva of the Later (Indo-Afghān) Gandhāra School. From the Kālawān Monastery at Taxila. National Museum of Pakistan, Karachi. Ht. 14 in. Marshall, *Taxila*, vol. I, pp. 338–9; vol. II, p. 470, no. 174; vol. III, pl. 137*c*.